SOCIO-LEGAL PROBLEMS IN RURAL HAITIAN ENVIRONMENT

A Major Cause of Haiti's Decadency

FIRST EDITION

Nixon A. Charles

ISBN 978-1-63784-205-8 (paperback)
ISBN 978-1-63784-206-5 (digital)

Hawes & Jenkins Publishing
16427 N Scottsdale Road Suite 410
Scottsdale, AZ 85254
www.hawesjenkins.com

Printed in the United States of America

CONTENTS

LIST OF TABLES AND FIGURES

Tables

Table 1: Evolution of agricultural exports from 1801 to 1818 in pounds

Product/year	1801	1809	1817	1818
Sugar	18518572	2320000	1800000	1900000
Coffee	43220270	22136392	20000000	20000000
Cotton	2480340	182917	40000	384000

Sources: Histoire Economique et Social D'Haïti de 1804 a nos jours by Bernardin E.

Table 2: Evolution of agricultural exports from 1819 to 1824 in pounds

Year/Product	Coffee	Cotton	Cocoa	Campeche	Mahogany*
1819	20280589	384001	326266	6717408	129962
1820	25192912	345341	435262	1870837	129509
1822	24235372	592368	464154	7470925	2622277
1824	44269084	1028045	461694	3767293	2181747

*feet

Table 3: Evolution of agricultural exports from 1827 to 1842 in pounds

Year/Product	Coffee	Cotton	Cacao	Sugar
1827	49662102	910768	702360	293970
1829	39968200	1019656	812895	46676
1831	40591817	1214238	330412	5114
1833	31602868	1755602	361438	379
1837	39845400	1013171	266024	21843
1842	40739061	880517	416827	6088

Table 4: Evolution of agricultural exports from 1842 to 1859 in pounds

Product/Year	Coffee	Cocoa	Cotton	Precious Wood
1842	40759064	416827	880517	19563147
1859	41712106	1397364	938056	88177600

Table 5: Evolution of agricultural exports from 1860 to 1864 in pounds

Product/Year	1860	1861	1862	1863	1864
Coffee	60514289	45660889	54779059	71712345	45168764
Mahogany	2264037	1659272	2441887	2016557	2369500
Cotton	668735	1139439	1437853	2217679	2237594
Cocoa	1582806	1394561	1743853	2338400	1399941

Table 6: Evolution of agricultural exports from 1842 to 1884 in pounds

Product/Year	1842	1859	1860	1864	1884
Coffee	40759064	41712106	60514289	45168764	74627236
Cotton	880517	938056	668735	2237594	1486146
Cocoa	416827	1397364	1581806	1399941	3156967

Sources: Report from Haitian Senate 1884–1885, Imprimerie l'Abeille, 1909

Table 7: Evolution of agricultural exports from 1950 to 1970 in metric tons

Product/Year	1950	1955	1960	1970
Coffee	40000	35000	38900	32000
Sisal	30000	35000	50000	19000
Sugar	53000	57192	54000	63900
Cocoa	2000			2900
Corn	203000	222000	226890	240000
Rice	28000	42000	41000	80000
Millet	173000	-	150000	210000
Plantain	247000	-	-	188860
Beans	1300000	50000	-	
Banana*	34300	-	-	40000
Cassava	104300	-	109600	130000
Cotton	3000	-	-	1750
Tabaco	500	700	1917	2200

Sources: FAO yearbook of production de 1950–1970

Table 8: Evolution of agricultural exports from 1960 to 1986 in metric tons

Year/Product	Coffee	Sisal	Sugar	Cocoa
1960	3900	50000	54095	
1970	32000	19000	63900	2900
1980	33250	17000	54434	2250
1986	28000	-	12000	2000

Sources: Histoire Economique et Social D'Haïti de 1804 à nos jours by Bernadin E.

PRELIMINARY OBSERVATION

Preliminary observation

The following text is an amplification of a thesis written and presented as a final work at the Law and Economics School of Gonaïves, an entity of the State University of Haiti, for the title of "Licentiate Ès Sciences Juridiques" in May 2001. Then it was believed that this work fulfilled a specific need for a given period; subsequent recommendations would aim, among other things, to strengthen agricultural production with a view to gradually and continuously improving the living conditions of a large part of the population that derives its livelihood directly or indirectly from agriculture.

However, with the January 12, 2010, earthquake that hit Port-au-Prince and its surroundings and that of August 14, 2021, in the south of the country and other natural disasters such as hurricanes and political upheavals such as the assassination of President Jovenel in July 2021, poor governance, and the glaring absence of an enlightened leadership, it is likely that the thesis defended in 2001 will still hold true, provided that the fundamental of the problems confronting the agricultural sector and the Haitian peasantry remains unchanged with profoundly dangerous variations. This approach contributes to the goal of enabling a broader audience to better understand the Haitian fray in a circumscribed and not global perspective because current natural disasters including recent earthquakes have shown the hideous spectacle of the deplorable living circumstances of most Haitians. These disasters have, moreover, put under the spotlight the face of a phantom public government incapable of covering up, as in the past, republican demagoguery.

In short, although these tragedies, especially the earthquake of January 12, 2010, have surely fanned the flames of universal humanism toward the Haitian people, they have mostly served to emphasize the inadequacy of Haitian authorities to take opportunities to propel this country forward.

A cursory review of Haitian administration over the past four decades reveals that the country's leaders have done everything possible to undermine the key economic and social balances that would ensure stability, peace, progress, and the liberation of the Haitian people. They have, on the other hand, led the country to total bankruptcy to the point where authentic Haitians hesitate to assert that our ancestors were not only the first to pose the problem of universal freedom but also the pioneers who shed their blood to prove—to the proponents of the first era of a savage capitalism based on the merciless exploitation of the Black people through slavery—that the fundamental human rights are sacred values inherent in the very existence of every human being.

Politically, the promise given in the aftermath of Jean-Claude Duvalier's removal from office in February 1986 swiftly turned into a nightmare because the new post-Duvalier's constitution adopted by the Haitian people by referendum on March 29, 1987, and what was to be considered as the plowshare of a new beginning for Haiti or the new social contract between the Haitians was quickly vilified and sabotaged by the supporters of the Duvalierist status quo and the newly elected president, Jean-Bertrand Aristide, and his team.

Remember the massacre of November 29, 1987? On that day, Haitian citizens peacefully lining up with their voter cards in hand to exercise their rights to vote were slaughtered by hundreds in voting centers by thugs of the army and the authorities who felt their hegemony was threatened; the elections were postponed and resumed only three years later. This made it possible for Father Jean-Bertrand Aristide to be elected president with a solid majority in both parliament and local governments. It was the perfect scenario that would allow a smooth start for the country by the application of the constitutional prescriptions in the formation of the new government and in the reorganization of existing institutions or in the establishment of new ones such as the electoral council, the office for the protection of citizens, the municipal and departmental assemblies, the interdepartmental assembly, and the constitutional court. It was also the ideal time to begin the process of reorganizing the public administration, upgrading the judicial system, and, above all, establishing of a policy oriented toward the implementation of a progressive and transformational program of the production system in the country to give hope to this population, which was ready to sacrifice itself to allow the nascent democracy to take shape.

Unfortunately, President Aristide, at the height of his popularity, chose, by ignorance or malice and/or by inexperience or pride, to depart from his organizational base, the parliament and his majority, to act as a sovereign with new heads, new collaborators, and new mercenaries of all stripes who opted for intimidation, violence, disorder, anarchy, and a style of government strangely reminiscent of most of those of the Haitian nineteenth century rather than adopting the political modernity that would pave the way for the emancipation of the Haitian people as defined by the constitution of March 29, 1987. Unfortunately, this experience was cut short by the coup d'état of September 29, 1991, orchestrated by the Haitian army. This coup d'état advocated the idea of a democratic correction by keeping the parliament in place to conceal the nature of the new power, which was inherently retrograde, corrupt, and bloodthirsty. The new authorities had dragged behind them a procession of dead bodies among President Aristide's supporters; the army created a terror rule throughout the country. Having been threatened from infancy by the administration of ex-president Aristide, the army, ironically, wrecked the democratic momentum it claimed to desire and to defend.

From his gilded exile in the United States and for having access to the money in the accounts of the Haitian government hold in US banks—that of TELECO, in particular—Aristide requested and obtained a total embargo on Haiti from the Organization of American States and then from the United Nations. It was the final straw for the Haitian middle class, which disintegrated and could no longer recover. During the approximately three years of the embargo, the Haitian economy was suffocated, subcontracting companies closed and moved to the Dominican Republic, the price of a gallon of gasoline increased from 15 to 245 gourdes, and the prices of basic necessities followed the process of disintegration of the country until President Aristide returned to power under the escort of more than twenty thousand American troops, who were to be replaced by contingency forces of United Nations under the MINUHA label.

This has never occurred in human history. Haiti was once again at the center of the global event. Hope and optimism were resurrected. The globe and those Haitians who believed in the idea of change were quickly disillusioned and disenchanted. Aristide, flanked by his international henchmen and local hawks, led a witch hunt with his political group "bo table la" then with his own Lavalas party, disregarding the constitution and Haitian laws. He would have the unwavering backing of influential members of the international community. Then international businessmen and representatives of some influential foreign politicians who assisted Aristide in regaining power landed in Haiti in the implementation of the Paris Agreement to capture all revenue-generating mines, state corporations, and other assets. Were we thus witnesses to all the unjust, nefarious, and pernicious plots that defied all logic for the coronation of René Préval as president in 1996 and, subsequently, for Aristide's return to power for a second term in 2001?

The Lavalas party would likely have the majority in parliament, and Aristide, despite a sharp decrease in his popularity, would be reelected with relative ease in the 2000 presidential election. However, Aristide and Préval and his team opted to present the public with one of the most abhorrent spectacles, which resulted in the theft of citizen ballots. Using their hold on the state apparatus, the Lavalasians, during the elections of May 21, 2000, set up an operation consisting of the replacement of the ballot boxes containing real votes with other ballot boxes containing tampered votes in favor of their candidates throughout the country. This operation was dubbed a "bat operation" by a politician of the time as it took place at the angelus throughout the night after the polling station closed. This massive operation of fraud undermined the electoral council, which had previously demonstrated a certain degree of seriousness and independence in relation to power; this heinous act prompted the intervention of the electoral council's president, who could not conceal his indignation by labeling this as a crime against Lez democracy. He requested a delay so he could examine the extent of the damage.

The response from the government was swift and immediate; it consisted of the mobilization of Lavalas, including ministers and senior public administration officials, police units, and members of the judiciary who had taken to the streets in pursuit of electoral council members who had denounced the situation. To prevent lynching by white-hot fanatics, the president and secretary general of the electoral council had to be removed from Haiti immediately, the former to the Dominican Republic en route to the United States and the latter directly to France. This environment of tension, intimidation, and fear had immobilized the country for several weeks, drove political opponents to gain the marquis, and essentially resulted to a quasi-dissolution of the *electoral council*. Thus, the Lavalas party became *hope killers*: corruption was rampant, opponents were suppressed or silenced, and political parties' headquarters and the homes of political opponents were torched.

It required a fresh intervention by the international community to halt Jean-Bertrand Aristide's slide and open the way for the second edition of Préval. At the end of Préval's term, this same international community had to intervene to designate Michel Martelly as president, preventing Préval from putting a member of his circle of vultures at the top of the Haitian government through fraudulent elections. Then, Martelly, like his predecessors, utilized public funds and corruption to pave the way for Jovenel, who, before his assassination and with the assistance of the international community, planted the death knell of the remaining Haitian public administrations. Consequently, institutions such as the parliament, the administration, and the judiciary, which formerly played a negligible front or vis-à-vis role, have ceased to exist entirely. The gangs that were in active gestation from the mid-1990s until 2005 or in marginal situations in the second half of the 2000s or in a state of alert when Michel Martelly was on the verge of losing power in 2014 really gained momentum after June 2018 when the fuel price was raised and Jovenel lost control of the government for more than a month. In compensation with the lack of popular support for the executive branch (the PHTK regime, Martelly's party), it appeared that the highest level of government devised a strategy to reactivate the gangs by reshaping them and by creating others across the country to intimidate the masses of the working-class neighborhoods and put an end to any protests against Jovenel's government.

From there, it became obvious: the real causes of the massacres that occurred in working-class neighborhoods, in La Saline on November 13–14, 2018, in Bel Air on November 4–5, 2019, and in Cité Soleil from May to July 2020. The silence of Jovenel Moïse's government on these massacres was shocking and complicit. Since then, gang leaders had dictated the norms; via blatant hypocrisy, the heads of state institutions assured impunity for the gangs, who, in turn, maintained their dominance by fostering an atmosphere of fear comprised of killings, rapes, kidnappings, ransoms, and other heinous crimes. Much better, and according to several sources, the suppliers and distributors of heavy weapons and ammunition to the gangs were individuals with strong ties to key international figures who formed or destroyed administrations in Haiti. Should one refer to the customs service's terms of reference on the control of products entering or departing a country through its ports, airports, borders, and entry gates to reduce doubts about such a claim?

In this unfavorable atmosphere, gangs proliferated in the country's metropolitan areas, flaunted their guns, confronted civilians, murdered bystanders, police officers, and others, and exposed or disposed of their remains on garbage heaps at the mercy of wild dogs and pigs. Occasionally, these gangs restricted access to several regions of the nation. For instance, the southern area of Haiti had been blocked off from the rest of the country for over a year due to the collusion of official authorities and two of the most prominent gang leaders, resulting in an untenable scenario for the country since the government no longer had a monopoly on lawful violence. Gangs were consequently so powerful that they could escape from their bosses within the government and the bourgeois' cycle. The combination of their armament and accumulated and dirty wealth provided them the freedom to behave as they chose by practicing mercenary alongside the abuses they did around the country. In addition, several gang leaders declared publicly that they seldom got orders or obeyed the commands of their superiors; they struck when they wanted and did what they wanted by stealing from the meager wallets of peasants, craftsmen, teachers, truckers, dealers, visitors, and others. Gangsters did not speak; they operated in the shadows. In Haiti, however, gang leaders regularly used social networks to gloat or proclaim that they had detained such and such an individual or that they would block such and such districts. Consequently, the gang bosses could not be caught or prosecuted since they were in conjunction with the country's government and closed business elite.

We note that the Haitian government was incapable of enforcing the base minimum of rules and social norms *that should govern life in society*. The excessive and constant impunity enjoyed by the gangs caused concern; a substantial segment of the Haitian populace opinion believed to be true that most of the heads of government and their ministers who had come to power since 2012 were the gangs' masterminds. Nonetheless, the lax and irresponsible response of the Haitian authorities to the insecurity that was devastating and destroying the country would be the catalyst for the proliferation of gangs in each of the country's cities, hamlets, villages, and suburbs.

In this context, it is evident that violence is, more than ever, the ideal tool for appropriating and preserving power in Haiti; whether you have been elected or appointed by any ruling Haitian government or by the international community, the results of your management of the country and the image you project of the country are irrelevant. These results will be worse than the disastrous precedents, and it repeats itself in an infernal and infinitesimal cycle.

The most important thing for Haitian officials is to be in power without a vision or a strategy to move the country forward except to serve a tiny group of individuals devoid of human essence and national sentiment. These officials with their tiny inner circles conceive of their existence as the accumulation of wealth through manipulation, cunning, and violence so that the others perish; these people view the nation as a corollary to their desire to maintain their claw and their will on state structures, even their demise through their descendants.

In less than forty years, Haiti has transformed itself from an exporter to an importer of food and agricultural products. Now Haiti has a rentier or counter economy. More than 75 percent of its consumption is imported. The country's inability to adapt to the first two industrial revolutions and modify its production structure have rendered its production system obsolete. Simultaneously, a rapine mindset has arisen around the Haitian leadership, which, unable to perform its regulatory function, places itself at the service of a tiny number of traditional bourgeois, who are now bolstered by newly arrived corrupt authorities. These interest groups seize Haiti in all its aspects by violence to the point of destroying all processes and legal tools available to public institutions to compel them to behave in a transparent manner for the common good. Imbued with a desire for quick profit, these interest groups pretend they favor a free market inside a capitalist economy, yet they work contrary to the market's functioning mechanism.

In Haiti, for instance, the markets for transport, the selling of products and services, and governmental contracts are extremely restricted; these fields of endeavor are reserved for a limited group of privileged individuals. No one else has access to it or can import similar things to sell as a businessman without political connections. In addition, information on the operation of these initiatives does not spread; interest groups and the government themselves prevent their dissemination. The price is not determined by the game of supply and demand. Neither is the authority responsible for defining the real tax base. Members of the privileged group keep for themselves all generating revenues activities. Public policy and monetary policy remain a pipe dream in this scenario. Furthermore, the government, through its officials, takes pleasure in pursuing sources of public finance via bilateral and international aid. Frequently, these officials fail to live up to their obligations; they sign contracts with the heads of foreign organizations who provide financial help at Haiti's detriment.

First, in 1980, on the advice of the American administration, the Haitian government slaughtered tens of millions of pigs in anticipation of an outbreak of swine flu that never materialized, destroying the livelihoods of hundreds of thousands of subsistent farmers who relied on pig farming. According to France's former minister of justice, Mrs. Christine Tabora, the Americans just sought to eliminate the competitiveness of highly demanded Haitian hog meat. Therefore, they utilized Haitian officials to eradicate the Haitian pig herd.

As early as 1987, under the label of structural adjustment, the Haitian authorities systematically eliminated customs restrictions by liberalizing markets, putting local products in competition with imported products that were substantially subsidized by the governments of their respective home countries. The producers in Haiti had no alternative but to cease the exploitation of their property as their income was far below their operational expenses. We recall the plight of Haitian rice farmers who faced competition from imported rice that was heavily subsidized by the United States in the 1990s. This circumstance has theoretically thrown more than two hundred thousand people out of work, including those whose livelihoods depended on the cultivation and sale of local rice. The same fate has befallen dairy products, oilseeds, coffees, cocoas, and bananas to the point that Haiti's agricultural production was virtually nonexistent.

Likewise, some public enterprises, such as TELECO, the "Cimenterie d'Haïti," and the "Minoterie d'Haïti," were coveted for their ability to generate substantial income in the context of the Paris Agreement between the presidency of Aristide, the World Bank, and certain masterminds of the international community. They were then recklessly liquidated at prices far below their market value. While the Haitian government might just reorganize them to make them far more productive, the bad management of these enterprises by the putschist regime should not justify firing tens of thousands of workers without warning or compensation. TELECO's case as an example is very revealing; this company was thriving even though it lacked back then a plan to satisfy an excess of more than one million subscription requests or to capture from this underserved market an upfront of more than 125 million dollars in connection costs, not including monthly fees and other related services. This corporation needed merely to raise its investment funds by appealing to public savings and to equip itself with an intelligent and energetic management whose decisions would be based on technical analysis of the economic and financial parameters rather than on the petty desire of a government head.

At the same time, certain Haitian governments incur exorbitant costs in the establishment of institutions that are ineffective and hence incapable of accomplishing their intended purposes. We might list as examples the CNE, the Caravan of Change, the BMPAD, the FDI, the Haitian Popular Bank, and the National Bank of Credit, among others. How many chances Haitian administrations have squandered by not having patriotic leaders who are serious, enlightened, competent, and infused with their mission and their obligation to put the nation's interests above those of clans and groups especially during the previous four decades? We recall the building proposal for the port of Fort-Liberté, which Michel Martelly rejected outright. The completion of this project would contribute to the amazing growth of the country's northern region. At the level of the windward canal, it would improve traffic and the movement of products and services and play a preponderant role in marine trade. By constructing new industrial and commercial infrastructures, it was going to bring about modernization. It was expected to generate a considerable number of employment and to contribute hundreds of millions of dollars each year into state coffers.

Unhappily, we are seeing the degeneration of the Haitian society and the polarization of an already volatile political life. The appointed or elected power holders, including those who, when not in power, pose as democratic, engage in undemocratic or even unpatriotic behavior; they transform the nation into a clan or family enterprise while speaking ironically and maliciously about election, democracy, political alternation, social peace, and development. Incapable of producing significant and consistent outcomes through reasonable initiatives and programs that would naturally qualify them for a second term in a democratic society, they resort to corruption and institutionalized violence to remain in power. They do not hesitate to suppress any local opposition that tries to confront this blind machine by maintaining a gloomy environment throughout an entire nation.

At this crucial juncture in our history as a nation, we must all appeal to civic conscience to erase dissension and replace it with unity and patriotism. As a result, it is crucial and essential to create a new government that, as the parliament is dysfunctional, would get its legitimacy from an agreement among the various sectors of the country in terms of its composition, mission, program, and length. Such a government will have greater discretion to tackle insecurity and foster an environment favorable to the conduct of elections. This government will need the support of the international community in the implementation, among other things, of a security plan aimed at purifying the police of corrupt agents through serious vetting to be able to track down the gangs that swarm in the country. This prerequisite is an essential condition for claiming to establish peace and stability.

Nonetheless, this new administration will first create an environment for a new social contract that would have the legitimacy of a consensus among the country's many sectors. Through efficient development processes, the new social compact would pave the path for the strengthening and stability of Haitian institutions because the need to reawaken the collective psyche of the Haitian people and to reshape the Haitian being through a transformative approach on the cultural, emotional, economic, social, environmental, architectural, urban, and productive levels are more pressing than ever before.

In addition to, and in parallel with, the emergency management consisting of finding the right formula to silence the gangs and restore the confidence of the affected population, it is necessary to arm oneself with the courage to abandon the ineffective model of the politico-legal system and *the Haitian economy.* A system that consistently and with minor variations seeks to perpetuate an oligarchy eager for hegemony without regard for the nation's greatest interests. A system that permits public property thieves and squanderers to be in the public eye without fear. A system that, despite the overwhelming quantity of crimes, has never been able to identify, judge, and punish a criminal. A system that views the honest individual as a deviant to be slain, ostracized, put down, or silenced. A system that promotes corruption as the path to royal achievement. A system that advocated a centralized government long before the Constitution of March 29, 1987, in opposition of it. Now, it is vital to combat impunity and clientelism in all its manifestations and to break with vertical power relations by establishing a decentralization-oriented process.

In conclusion, it will be necessary to lay the foundations of a transparent policy that should lead to the complete elimination of the politico-legal economic system of the "ownership society" style; this system, which has cleverly concealed its ugliness and cruelty for more than two centuries, widens the gulf between the decision-makers and the excluded by destroying the middle class and siphoning off the country's assets, leaving the peasantry in the most abject conditions because it would never have exposed the irresponsibility, inconsistency, and ambivalence of Haiti's political and economic leadership prior to January 12, 2010, and, even more so, throughout the preceding fifteen years.

This administration will need to construct a plan for economic recovery and an atmosphere that promotes the bourgeois' ideals of frugality and hard labor. According to some analysts, the present situation in Haiti would likely necessitate a five-year rehabilitation plan costing around eight billion dollars per year. As corrective and preventive measures are needed to avoid repeating the same errors in providing help to Haiti, it is essential to incorporate an investment and guarantee fund in the rebuilding plan. This fund—in contrast to that of the OPIC, which served (in conjunction with the return to power in 1994 of former president Jean-Bertrand Aristide) only a small, restricted circle of traditional Haitian investors (bankers, importers, dealers, and manufacturers, among others)—will consist of promoting the emergence of new local, departmental, and regional economic partners by ensuring the promotion and establishment of new companies in various fields across the country. This will result in the establishment of steady jobs that will prevent people from migrating to large cities where human conditions are already dire.

In addition, the implementation of the recovery plan in terms of the construction or repair of infrastructure such

as roads, schools, bridges, public buildings, social housing, and land use planning must be based on new norms
and standards that are accepted by Haitian experts and are
legally enforceable. From there, a comprehensive strategy
for the repair and development of the land will emerge.

This administration will be accountable for paving the
road so that in the medium and long term, Haitian authority will avoid hiding reality to confront the development
question in terms of internal inequality, social dynamics,
and capital flows. We must not lose sight of the fact that the
salvation of Haiti will depend, in part, on the implementation of a land policy and recapitalization programs aimed,
in part, at agro-industries; the development and implementation of policies for public security, public health, education, promotion of culture and universal human rights;
road and telecommunications infrastructure; investment
and employment; housing; and the environment.

For Haiti to rise from the ashes, cease to be the pariah
of the world, and put its genius to the service of its people,
it is essential to clearly establish and rationally exploit the
resources of the soil and of the Haitian subsoil to integrate
into economic production the excluded, the peasant and
urban masses, and to support a space of law that is respect-
ful of freedoms, promotes republican values, and is concerned with a good organization of the global productive.

PREFACE

After a bachelor of science in international management from the American College of Switzerland in July 1990, I enrolled at the Gonaïves law school in the State University of Haiti in November 1991. *Since then, our passion for legal sciences has continued to rise and take part of our mind.* And, after having taken courses in both economy and rural law at both Port-au-Prince and Gonaïves law schools and having seen the evolution of the Haitian countryside from infancy as exit work, we desired to write about rural region of Haiti and its evolution over time. The choice of our subject became clearer when we saw through the threshold of the third millennium that Haiti has been facing a dilemma, which is to achieve its food self-sufficiency demands while still adhering to the recommendations of the international community through the economic plan of Bretton Woods Institutions.

At this juncture, the implementation of an agricultural development plan is more than necessary in view that the country is experiencing problems in domains that intersect in reacting negatively upstream and downstream on the agricultural production. The situation is so serious and dangerous that some experts believe that

1) in Haiti, it appears that emotions dominate thinking and equality before the law is the exception;

2) the Haitian economy is on the verge of collapse, anemic, and asphyxiated by imbalances generated from scratch before and during the embargo imposed by the international community in Haiti following the coup d'état on September 30, 1991;

3) Haitian agriculture is at its lowest level while latent or declared conflicts between property owners or alleged property owners have been institutionalized in some parts of the country;

4) the balance of payments accuses a deficit that households are compelled to cover and bear as the Haitian government strives to propose new taxes that reduces the already vulnerable household daily basket;

5) unemployment reached an unprecedented record level even in the rural area;

6) since abduction has become a new kind
of crime in Haiti, the level of insecurity
is at an all-time high;

7) impunity is the rule: criminals roam
the streets in full sight of everybody
without being worried;

8) corruption is legion;

9) education continues to be diverted
from its purpose; and

10) youth are left to fend for themselves:
in the absence of role models, they
mistakenly adopt alien conduct and
bizarre attitudes in violation of Haitian
norms and expertise.

In this context, we had scrutinized the entire Haitian experience under both legal and socioeconomic angles and the evolution of the international world through its *north–south* facet: a national agricultural program that focuses on investment of capital in agricultural production, revaluation of cultivated and cultivable farmland, and functional training in the rural area at the intent of farmers and the first level agricultural technicians to better adapt the legal framework thereon toward an improvement of agricultural production in Haiti.

In summary, if we made the autopsy of the wound that plagues Haitian agriculture—by identifying the origin and causes of agricultural issues in the country—we would be able to propose or provide remedies. Thus, the community approach seems to be the most appropriate to highlight the vast potential of Haiti to increase its agricultural production.

Through our efforts, we have endeavored to place in the hands of the decision-makers avenues and tracks of reflection for a more effective management of agriculture and the Haitian countryside. This work could be expanded and repolished so that agricultural policies in Haiti be the product of a collection of well-written ideas and implemented concepts that reflect the rural reality and its improvement and what Haiti could achieve with its countryside.

ACKNOWLEDGMENT

We gratefully acknowledge the assistance of

Professor Mécène JEAN-LOUIS, a former judge at the Haitian Supreme Court who had accepted the direction of this work by guiding us through with great kindness by his remarks and judicious advice.

My parents, Mrs. and Mr. Alix Charles Céus, who left for beyond respectively in 2014 and 2017 and who, during their lifetime, had a thousand and one times followed the gesture of the pelican, sacrificing and depriving themselves of the minimum even when the harvests were not good to pay for my studies, may the eternal light enlighten them and they rest in peace.

My caring wife, Fedline and our two sons, Fedgy and Mike, may God's light and wisdom transcend you and allow you to always be my ideal landmark in good and bad days. I dedicate these lines to you as a testimony of my great love and my deepest gratitude.

INTRODUCTION

In 1789, a revolution undermined the foundations of old French monarchy and abolished the privileges of the nation's aristocracy and clergy. Less than a year later, following several failed efforts, Saint-Domingue (a French colonial territory that became independent as Haiti) raised the flag of rebellion trying to build a new social order and an independent nation.

The 1791 upheaval at Paris and other parts in France had to create in this colonial territory a multifaceted revolution. First, this revolution was anti-colonialist with the slave's owner's movement, anti-segregationist with mulattocs' movement, and anti-slavery with slaves' movement. The French revolution of 1789 was a response to tax inequality, injustice, royal despotism, and the economic, social, political, and religious crisis. The Saint-Domingue revolution would not be possible if the prerequisites of this explosion were not met.

Saint-Domingue's revolution was born under the contradictions and inconsistencies of an exploitation system that were too greedy and could not find on time the ideal formula to satisfy the aspirations of a colony tired of colonialism rigors. That revolution was also sparked by inherent and internal contradictions within Saint-Domingue social categories at the time. These contradictions constituted the source of various social conflicts that will shake the foundation of the exploitation system and annihilate slavery at Saint-Domingue.

But these contradictions seem to persist even today in Haiti, which has been severely impacted by political, cultural, environmental, and socio-economic disaster. Haiti, largely considered as an agricultural country, is still looking for itself. To date, at the beginning of twenty-first century, Haiti, exposed to agricultural failure and poor governance, is still unable to provide to its population with a minimal quality of life through agricultural self-sufficiency. Its rural and suburban populations suffer from serious food shortages while in highland surrounding Port-au-Prince and in certain other towns, a very, very tiny number of individuals live like lords from the Middle Ages and oil barons or royalty from the old dynasties or the great dynasties. What an absurdity, and wouldn't it be important to investigate the causes and nature of this profound imbalance, which is, of course, both economic and social but also legal in the sense that it will necessitate a review of Haitian legislation to discover the flaws and gaps that impede the development of the countryside where peasants appear doomed to remain stagnant? Is the relevant Haitian legislation excessive, insufficient, or unenforceable in regard with the customs and manners that characterize the Haitian countryside? Consequently, one appeals to the Haitian life experiences by asking as Montesquieu did: is the law not derived from the nature of things? This is what influenced and motivated the choice of our thesis: *Understanding Haiti's Poverty through Socio-Legal Problems in the Peasant Milieu.*

At this point, we proceeded with an analysis of the universal world, the Haitian reality, and the Haitian particularity by referring to relevant documentation, programs, and economic projects using the laws and codes focused on development of rural environment in Haiti and interviewing some historical data or current events toward the evolution and progression of all rural entity-related activities. However, President Boyer's period (1825–1843) will serve as a terminus a quo since the first legal document directly connected to the Haitian rural world especially the one relating to agriculture was born during that time; the fact remains that, if required, we shall appeal to events that occurred before 1825. Similarly, for the terminus ad quem, the eightieth years will be of great interest because, on the one hand, they correspond to the end of the development assistance program to Haiti and, on the other hand, they highlight the peak of the agricultural sector decline and deterioration of the Haitian rural world.

Therefore, it is evident that the word "agricultural self-sufficiency" used above is by essence associated with the social sciences and the economics. However, if we consider the Roman adage *"ubi societas, ibi ius,"* it is both intriguing and interesting to approach the problem legally. It is imperious that the Haitian legislature has always accorded a prominent place to the regulations of agricultural sector, which is the primary occupation of the peasantry, the basis of the Haitian economy, and the main taxation source for the government. In addition, we want to address this issue because it involves the Haitian man, its immediate environment, which is the farmland, his daily life, and the type of socio-legal organization on his farm, taking into consideration the unfortunate and negative influence of the global environment on Haitian policy and life.

It would be odd not to recollect the documentation issues we experienced. Due to the rarity of publications presenting a variety of perspectives on topics comparable to ours (Internet did not exist at the time), it was essential to exercise patience and courage to obtain the bare minimum of knowledge—what we have achieved.

This work was designed, constructed, and organized to fully comprehend the social and legal origins of the decline of Haitian agriculture and to gain a better understanding of the poor development of our rural areas to determine what could still be done legally, technically, and socially to achieve at least agricultural self-sufficiency to ensure, among other things, the emancipation of the Haitian peasantry.

For this purpose, we devised a plan for information-collecting mostly based on structural analysis. In this regard, we have continued with the documentary inquiry, as stated previously. To examine the ensuing effects on agriculture, emphasis was placed on the level of conformity between the practices and traditions of Haitian peasants and the relevant legislative documents. Thus, we were able to locate pertinent material to further our job.

Our work has two main parts: the first part is entitled "Incidence of Internal and External Historical Facts on Haitian Rural Paysage" and the second part is called "Farmland: Legal Aspects versus US and Customs in the Haitian Countryside." Each part is divided into two chapters, which are respectively subdivided into two sections.

The first chapter, entitled "Overview of the Situation," describes life in the Haitian countryside from independence to the present day, thereby highlighting the origins of Haitian underdevelopment and the self-centeredness that has always characterized the political and administrative elite in relation to the nation and the peasantry.

In the second chapter, "Economic Development Policy," the focus was placed on Haiti's human development in relation to that of developed or comparable nations.

However, the results demonstrated that it was, in this regard, above the average of less developed nations despite a decline in satisfying dietary requirements. It should be mentioned that the worsening of the sociopolitical crisis accompanied by natural disasters over the last fifteen years has drastically changed living conditions in Haiti with negative impacts on human development in this country. Much better, Haiti confronts neoliberalism through structural adjustment forced by multinational investors, whose fundamental character is a challenge—as individuals from Third World nations—of meager social benefits that have a profound impact on rural areas.

In the third chapter, "Impacts Succession Regulations on Agriculture," we put in relief the legal and social difficulties that confronts the Haitian agriculture despite the vital role that it plays in the distribution of wealth and the social balance in the country.

In the fourth chapter, we have analyzed the legal texts directly related to the management of agricultural land to determine their weight in the development of Haitian agriculture through the role the local authorities will have to play as spearhead (Constitution of 1987) of a ten-year phased program for agricultural development.

Therefore, must we admit that the rural Haiti has suffered more from the legacy of French colonialism, the grip of Western dominant policy on Haiti, the primacy of customary law, and the absence of adequate agricultural structures, poor governance, land degradation, and lack of investment in this sector?

We infer from the preceding that a more just and equitable society is required in Haiti. Today, it is realistic to choose an all-encompassing development that satisfies the desires of all Haitians.

PART 1

Incidence of Internal and External Historical Facts on Haitian Rural Paysage

CHAPTER 1

OVERVIEW OF THE SITUATION

Haiti has reached a point in its history where most of its population is the combination of the refusal of a lawlessness state and the desire for a true takeoff through an economic growth and a financial development, but Haiti recognizes itself. It is helpless to accomplish and implement the necessary changes, either resigning or rebelling.

If underdevelopment is visible to all, its historical and social causes are unknown or poorly understood. Some are less influenced in their everyday lives than others; reasons and consequences are involved. But what is becoming increasingly apparent is the need to minimize socio-economic isolation, release the energy of all social actors, create civil society, restore the dignity of the Haitian man, and restore citizen freedoms.[1]

The requirement for a global development necessitates a larger role for the government and may not be satisfied in the long run. If most of Haitian people choose to act in their own best interests, they must construct their actions

---

[1] *Bulletin Justice Economique*, 5eme no. January 1998.

on strong foundations: law and order. This is the historical moment's reasoning.

Section 1: History of the state and development in Haiti

1.1. Negritude as heritage

From the proclamation of our independence, Haitian leaders faced a double challenge consisting of overcoming racial divisions caused by slavery between Whites, Mulattoes, and Blacks and erecting an independent and sovereign country that would be able to stand up to the great colonial powers and refuse any form of foreign dominance.

First, Dessalines had to declare that "all Africans or Indians as well as their descendants were eligible to become Haitians"[2] and "no White man, whatever their nationality, set foot in the territory as a master or owner, and will be allowed to acquire in the future any type of property." To clear until the last symbol of the European idol, Dessalines ordered

---

[2] Fourth article of *Imperial Constitution* of 1805.

the killing of all the French persons who remained on the island with the idea of overthrowing the newly established order and demanded that every Haitian vow on the altar of the nation: rather die than live under the domination.

Secondly, Dessalines—upon becoming the sole master of the country—compelled the former slaves to perform labor on the enormous farms shared by the Mulatto and Black generals of the new army. Aboriginal cultural traditions will be cursed as voodoo leaders will be punished relentlessly.

Besides the statements and practices claiming to affirm the fiercest national independence, another reality will gradually become consistency: the marginalization of the masses of newly liberated by the new state power around the state. In fact, a privileged class declared to be the nation's exclusive spokesman. Then, in the most national creeds, the Haitian nation would drift like a hopelessly lost object.

The most intransigent social demands from the newly liberated would soon emerge refusal of drudgery, refusal to produce export commodities, claim the right to property and landownership, the right to free movement within the country, etc.

On the political and literary stage, however, all these social concerns were veiled under a shared racial vocabulary created by a privileged class as Black as Mulattoes. The history of Haiti would not be an eternal replay of racial differences. Were Mulattoes or Blacks more likely to run the country?

The Mulatto oligarchy believed they were qualified to run the nation because they viewed themselves as relatives of the White proprietors who fled the country or perished during the revolution. On the other side, the Black generals asserted that they were the actual representatives of the masses, which made up most of the country, and that they must assume leadership.

Therefore, in the late nineteenth century, the two major parties (created on a patronage basis) dominating the country corresponded to two trends based on two colorist ideologies: the National Party where Blacks recognized themselves and the Liberal Party that gathered Mulattos; despite that, both parties included Blacks and Mulattoes.

1.2 Ambivalence of political elite toward the peasantry

On this premise, any representation of the Haitian country would be stolen by a traditional elite who desired to differentiate and oppose themselves as far as possible to the people (particularly those from rural regions) who were accused of being superstitious and stupid. Therefore, it was necessary to wipe the masses off the political scene in the spirit of what was termed "social peace" in the 1940s and especially when Dumarsais Estimé was elected president by the Haitian legislature on August 16, 1946. However, Estimé's administration had done all possible to foster the ascent of descendants of former slaves who had become weary of languishing in ignorance and debasement.

At the same time, as the world was becoming more civilized, there was a growing desperation for recognition; thus, the anti-racist movement would continue to confront the racism trap. The questioning of despotism and the omnipotence of the heads of state whose practices were modeled on those of the slave masters were avoided: the independence heroes, Black intellectuals, and statesmen were celebrated in literature as the only ones capable of producing the redemption of the discriminated negroes.[3]

Ensure that no Haitian identity was assumed. It was evidenced by the measures of the government to control and restore to the mediocrity the masses of impoverished peasants, landless, and uneducated, who were kept out of the cities and away from the political scene.

---

[3] Trouillot, Michel-Rolph. *Les Racines Historiques de l'Etat duvalerien.* Edition H. Deschamps, 1985.

This program was implemented to retain the hegemony of a selfish oligarchy, which was hesitant to put its whole position into play and even less prepared to pay for its hegemony with the bourgeois' ideals of austerity and hard labor. Therefore, they preferred to contribute to the exercise of caste, turning their backs on the interests and realities of the country by caulking in the cities for the sole purpose of monopolizing what the army and the civil administration could offer as sinecures and strategic positions from which they could attract a substantial portion of the trade benefits, the majority of which was delegated to foreign consignees' traders established in the various ports of the county. This observable tendency from 1804 was manifested in the Rural Code of 1826, also known as the Rural Code of Boyer, which had systematically oppressed the country's farmers by instituting a kind of serfdom for the benefit of the national nobility. Under these circumstances, with this elite permanently relegated to parasitism, Haiti was enveloped in underdevelopment and with individualism, tyranny, caste or class prejudice, and a lack of disinterestedness[4] as its backdrop.

Section 2: Peasantry in front of the state

In the first years following Haiti's independence, the military elite grabbed plantations, land, farms, and plants; partnered with traders; and appropriated the country for their own use; barring small farmers and attempting to enforce a colonial-era labor pattern on the plantations. But the peasantry of former slaves expressed its liberation in terms of autonomy of the worker on his land by establishing familial gardens that replaced old places to live during the colonial era and were nicknamed headlines teeth because they had been nibbled by machete on the edge of large estates owned by city-dwelling absentee owners. In addition, the peasantry refused to be bribed again on the plantations, which quickly began to fall because of the restructuring of global markets.[5]

---

[4] Dr. Bernardin, Ernst. *Histoire Economique et Sociale d'Haïti de 1804 à nos jours.* Imprimeur II, 1998.

[5] "What authors call the victory to the wear and tear of the small peasantry on the layers of the country who had opted for the great property."

2.1 The exclusion of peasantry by the state

Throughout the nineteenth century, wealthy landowners and merchants routinely extracted agricultural earnings from peasant labor. This was made feasible by taxing export commodities and by taxing imported agricultural inputs and commodities, with the government's active backing for the export sector and the participation of European and American proponents of free trade.

However, small farmers defended their food production method and particular farms. The country—a stormy alliance of military, proprietors, and merchants—was an impediment to progress because it was only unstable because of weak governance. Prior to the French Revolution of 1789, Haiti, formerly known as Saint-Domingue, was the most productive country in the world, but its economy had since plummeted. It unfortunately became dependent for half of its commerce on the United States. Haiti—which was supposed to be an exporter of agricultural products—already imported more agricultural items and their derivatives than any other nation. Even the dominant classes shifted their focus away from agriculture and toward commerce and finance. In doing so, they compounded the country's financial loss.

At the turn of the century, the merchants of the waterfront of Port-au-Prince, who had been briefly displaced by the Syrian-Arab invasion of Haiti, were firmly entrenched. During the American occupation (1915–1934), the administration was more centralized, the army was upgraded to quell peasant rebellions, and huge foreign corporations were favored and protected throughout the country.

The ineffective and inadequate model of export economy of raw commodities and food production widened the gap between the affluent and the poor, policymakers and the excluded, and the centralizing state and the bare minimum of civil society. Vertical relations of power and patronage, intensified tensions between Blacks and Mulattoes, and between towns and countries all contributed to the overall compartmentalization of the Haitian society, which was confronting the expanding centralization of the country. This was the manifestation of a civic society that was still in its infancy and should stay so for some time.

In addition, the demographic equilibrium was shattered with increased land demand and stagnant agricultural production. Many young people were unable to remain on farms and in rural areas. The levies on agriculture, which accounted for most of the ruling classes and the government's revenues, were no longer permitted to support the expanding population of nonproducers. The extremely low level of income and property transfer from the government and the rich to the poor in the city and rural were under jeopardy.

From 1957 through 1986, the great disintegration of the country ultimately settled these violent or latent tensions. At that time, which was characterized as unstable and dictatorial, the Haitian government became totalitarian rather than the usual authoritarian State.[6]

2.2 Low productivity

Beginning in the 1950s, major development projects had emerged; a noticeable one was the Development Agency of Artibonite (ODVA). However, most of these projects failed to address the fundamental actions and conditions that would enable the rural world to evolve.[7] As a result of the community's techniques of integrated growth throughout the seventies, the Haitian peasantry could barely maintain its production system due to insecurity on farmland and concerns about the future. Thus, productivity continued to decline.

However, some modernization of the country took place during the thirty years of dictatorship from 1957 to 1986, includ-

---

[6] Trouillot, Michel-Rolph. Les Racines Historiques de l'Etat duvalerien, Edition H. Deschamps, 1985.

[7] "Despite the fact that the Inter-American Committee of the Alliance for Progress has lent more than \$320 million to Haiti from 1972 to 1982 in parallel with the increase in external aid."

ing the construction of roads and the international airport or the establishment of industrial units, but at the expense of the loss of human resources, the marginalization of the peasantry, the suffocation of the province, and the institutionalized corruption and perversion of the country.

Financing due to foreign assistance had ceased for twenty years, and due to mistrust of the Mulatto bourgeoisie, all initiatives that could have taken the middle class—falsely invested for the sake of Blackness ideology—that was invested to the mission to rehabilitate the country did not last long. To the disadvantage of the people, exploitable mineral resources were stolen by foreign corporations and a few Haitian allies. The farmland itself up to the hills was overexploited beyond its potential for regeneration, resulting in a significant decline.

In such context, the results had been catastrophic: the rural population had been increasingly in difficulty to survive from its work on the farmland; a rapidly growing part of the population in search for work was massed or packed in sub-human conditions in cities especially in Port-au-Prince; and the environmental degradation in many areas had reached the point of no return.

The establishment of factories for subcontracting semimanufactured prod-ucts for export, despite creating fifty thou-sand jobs, monopolized electrical energy from Péligre, exacerbated polarization between the capital and the provinces, and ultimately resulted in a substantial repatriation of profits by foreign investors. Consequently, the deployment of these industries had rarely benefitted the whole nation. Contrary to the legislation con-trolling the topic, the Haitian bourgeoi-sie had limited investment in these enter-prises with outsiders, notably Americans, holding the overwhelming share.

2.3 Chronic underdevelopment

Tragic is the outcome of the previous two centuries about the growth of Haiti, the role of money power, the function of the government, and most people who cannot make a livelihood through their job. It tells us that leaving progress to the initiative of foreigners or a minority group that dominates the country is unacceptable. The history of our country—not just the history taught in schools—has proven that this minority group, already privileged by both its ability to make decisions and its affluence, tends to grow its market share at the expense of the overwhelming majority, curiously to its own harm thereafter.

Briefly, we have on our hands an underdeveloped country; this phrase being taken both in relation to more developed or industrialized countries such as the Dominican Republic or the United States and France, as well as in comparison to what Haitians themselves would consider Haiti to be.

Rich individuals who were born and raised in a city have little understanding of how peasants and tens of thousands of families in disadvantaged areas live. Yet, like them, they aim to a degree of equilibrate food, health, comfort, safety, and space that is not necessarily the bare minimum but a minimum that is respectable and does not create shame. However, this level is becoming increasingly unattainable, and poverty is growing relentlessly. Consequently, poverty is spreading to formerly charming and attractive districts, where household unit rentals are increasing despite a drastic deterioration in living conditions and where two or more people are living in dwellings built for one. In shantytowns and cardboard cities, the living and health conditions remain untenable.

This daily humiliation endured by countless Haitians makes us all filthy, and imperceptibly, beautiful places such as the waterfront or seaside of Port-au-Prince, Jérémie or Cap-Haitien, became garbage dumps: potholed and congested streets, crippled buildings, dozens of women and children fight for a trickle of water escaping from a broken pipe, sick meat or flies-wrapped fruits and vegetables sit next to trash or garbage in clear violation of Articles 22[8] and 23[9] of the Constitution of March 29, 1987.

Does this repulsive spectacle excite the bourgeois housewife as much as the street seller or taxi driver? No. However, it has been deteriorating for decades. Since 1986 and especially since 1991, the escalating crisis has aggravated this scenario even if it did not cause it.

Haiti's hills contain barely 2 percent of their original forest cover. Despite their own efforts, the peasants can no longer preserve their primary labor tool, which is farmland. They hacked down trees to create charcoal, leaving the field vulnerable to tropical storms that eroded the planting area.

Once again, farmer organizations are seeking cash to purchase mechanical equipment, fertilizer, and seeds. Communities collaborate to build their own water sup-

---

[8] "The State recognizes the right of every citizen to decent housing, education, food and social security."

[9] "The State is obliged to ensure to all citizens, in all the territorial collectivities, the appropriate means to guarantee protection, maintenance, and restoration of their health by the creation of hospitals and health centers."

ply networks. The workshops will revolve around a parish or artisan cooperative.

Surely, we all require beauty. Even if we are impoverished, we are all human, uncomfortable with hardship and proud of our decency. No matter how filthy and unhealthy our living circumstances are, we want our daily lives to be as attractive and enjoyable as possible.

How then might this transition be achieved? How to avoid misleading us? What tactics have other developing nations followed? And what have been the primary topics sponsored by international organizations over the previous few decades? And what objectives should we pursue with economic development policy?

CHAPTER 2

POLITICAL ECONOMY OF DEVELOPMENT

Prior to World War II, the specialization of nations and regions in the worldwide division of economic activity was accepted as a natural consequence of laissez-faire. The example of China, this vast nation with its people and its history, and the advent of new nations of the third world have made it possible to inquire about development in terms of internal inequities, social dynamics, and capital flows.

As a result, there has been an increase in research on the fundamental manifestations of underdevelopment, such as the heterogeneity of developing nations, their trade dependence vis-à-vis other nations, and the too-slow diffusion of technical progress and innovation throughout all their social strata. Despite these achievements in the field, we most frequently view development through the lens of poverty's symptoms.

Section 1: Human development

In this regard, though, the world has advanced. It shifted from global economic metrics such as the gross national product per capita to specific indicators of satisfaction of everyone's fundamental needs[10]

1.1 Indicators of human development in Haiti

Human development indicators for Haiti—compared with those in the Caribbean region (the Dominican Republic, in particular) and those of the industrialized countries in terms of natural data (life expectancy and food requirements expressed in calories) or demographic (percentage of population in school by age and with access to drinking water) or economic or values commonly used by the wealthiest countries—had improved significantly over the last twenty or thirty years before the year of 2001 and until 2010:

1. The income of industrialized nations are roughly twenty times

---

[10] "This is the human development approach of the United Nations Development Program."

than those of the least developed nations (LDC or PMA).

2. Haiti achieves a human development somewhat above the LDC average but with a decline in food security.

3. In comparison to the Dominican Republic, Haiti is inferior in every respect.

4. Regardless of the principles respected in other nations, Haitian children are frequently the victims. Although they are the future, they lack education.

This circumstance does not illustrate the enormous financial differences and other facilities enjoyed by the wealthy and the impoverished in all nations and in Haiti, in particular. This disparity is 140 times greater in underdeveloped nations than in developed nations. It does not demonstrate a difference in treatment between girls and women and boys and men.

The figures shown here, like all numbers do, are statistical; that is, they do not consider individuals or small groups. Based on the human development approach of the United Nations, Haiti should look for a development that will help as many people as possible, if not everyone. Everyone will be affected if Haitian people do not limit themselves to a specific quantity in absolute terms. Certainly, if they set themselves some goal, such as at least 40 percent of rural students completing at least middle school throughout the first decade of the 2000s and at least 90 percent of the rural population having access to potable water close to their homes, there is still plenty to be done.[11]

However, if states, governments, and international organizations define objectives, it is to plan the activity and advance with greater certainty. Consequently, Haitian people must formulate these

---

[11] "Human development is therefore a broader set of development factors than economic development alone. These indicators, although imperfect, allow us to better understand how the country and the world consider the totality of their population."

objectives in the most realistic manner feasible, considering the actual possibilities of action. The indicators help specifically to compare the results to the objectives as the development moves forward, ensuring the results still are accurate.

1.2 Participative leitmotif approach to development

Managers, members of the educated classes, and decision-making apparatus who get their incomes and status on decisions made on behalf of others have the highest obligation to speak the truth. In the meanwhile, those with lesser education should endeavor to get a deeper understanding of the economic and social concerns around how and why other individuals and organizations earn a living, how to divide profits and responsibilities, and where and in what sequence to prioritize reforms.

In the absence of restrictions, complicity between leaders and citizens is required for a democratic growth requiring the involvement of the general populace. People must thus not only learn but also speak out: say things daily from rural and shady locations in newspapers, cassettes, on air, and social media and let the world know that Haiti exists.

The practical training in civic and economic problems should be the focal point of Haiti's growth. It is hoped that trained professionals are working to carry out these responsibilities, paving the way for pedagogical action to create the rule of law and democratic freedom in Haiti.

Section 2: Current ideological constraints

2.1 Events in production reports

Finally, the principles of arbitrary dictatorship have been shattered in the contemporary world. The economic and social growth of three European nations lately liberated from dictatorships have advanced significantly because it appears that in a democratic environment, the freedom of people is more congruent with market forces; Spain, Portugal, and

Greece have been really altered during the past four decades.

As for the former countries subject to communist influence and Soviet dependence, their development is significantly more differentiated; this is since the dirigisme in the settlement of production report by the center or authorities does not prepare them for the harsh individual law of Western capitalism. If the rule of law exists in the texts, it cannot effectively govern the powerful new economic forces that invest in these nations, the new "farthest east" of Europe.

We observe the similar pattern in Argentina. Massive inflows of foreign capital, in search of exorbitantly high interest rates, purchase shares of state-owned corporations, diverting their focus from domestic purposes for export. There is a need to meet the demand for equipment or basic commodities among the middle and lower classes.

Once the boom and the rush for large financial gains ended, these investors fled the nation, leaving a whole sector in ruins. Again, it is the fragility of the rule of law that leaves the subject open to conjecture.[12] Civil society is still searching for a representation of actual nations in Latin America's political organizations.

The Cuban example likewise requires thoughtful consideration. After gaining independence from Spain, a colonial power, and the United States, a neocolonial power, this nation has increased the welfare and education of its entire population, widened access to public services, and gained the respect of nations but at the expense of individual liberties and another dominance, which was strategic procurement and capital from the Soviet Union.

It is via enlightened authoritarianism and the personification of power that the government's restrictive will has been communicated here. However, the great-

---

[12] "What the Economist Fritz Deshommes calls Latin America: The Lost Decade of the 1980s where the most visible manifestations of the economic crisis were felt by the application of the neoliberal precepts."

est error made by Cuban officials was failing to diversify the economy away from sugar, leaving them without adequate space (despite the tourism boom) when the sugar supply ceased. As a form of punishment for the Cuban people's naive confidence in their leader, US diplomacy then closed the trap of the embargo on this country, which had led so naturally to commerce with the United States.

A similar dilemma emerges about the enlightened dictatorships such as those that have enabled Taiwan and South Korea to accomplish their remarkable economic growth during the past three decades. This is the question of the justification of a state that—through illegitimate means, that is, by severely restricting more or less freedoms—achieves in a generation results that more or less benefit all layers of the population, first in terms of satisfaction of basic needs and then (relatively recent in the case of Taiwan, the state of siege was lifted in 1992; it had been imposed in 1950!) in terms of the exercise of freedoms.[13]

Without doubting the economic results, it must be questioned if they might not have been obtained at a cheaper cost through freedom or if they justify the enormous environmental disaster. The history of these nations likely compelled them to adopt this sort of strategy (war in Korea or perpetual threat of war in Taiwan). In addition, their geostrategic position renders them impervious to economic reprisals from the West. However, the truth remains that these two nations have deftly evaded the harsh capitalist paradigm (which is also warped in some other places compared to the thought of its founders). They discovered their own way to growth.

Actually, to make the comparison with Haiti, the question does not emerge in the same terms due to the country's history and international restraints from its inception. Haiti is on the doorstep of the

---

[13] Ibid.

world's first superpower. Haiti has always been rescued from dictatorship by discernible and non-negligible international intervention. The dictatorship did not assist the country to advance or flourish economically; rather, it contributed to the social decline of a whole generation. Since 1492, our history has been significantly impacted by foreign limits, as evidenced by the memory of ancient times!

2.2 The New World order

Since the colonial nations attained their independence in the 1960s, development has been a popular term among international organizations. The imperialists claimed it for so long with peace and disarmament; today, the struggle is with free trade and increasingly with democracy, privatization, and world market integration.

As governments follow one another and decades pass, so do the concepts advanced by great nations. After years of aid being squandered by corrupt governments of poor nations and lobbyists from the world's superpowers, the hard core of developed nations vis-à-vis the underdeveloped countries has become a real policy of adjustment, which intends to support the institutions of Bretton Woods (International Monetary Fund [IMF] and World Bank) in their recovery of aid funds.

While these institutions exhibit democratic characteristics, they fail to promote political changes anytime they help to enhance stability. Since the debt crisis of the early 1980s, there has been no development aid for developing nations if they do not embrace ultracapitalism and democratic values (although, for the latter, the interpretations are permissive).

2.2.1 The predominance of economy

Under the guise of rationality, any ideology, diffused by the West and adopted by nearly all regions of the world, is characterized by the mechanization principle: the means that men use to achieve their goals are geared toward the ultimate goal, and each social activity is evaluated in terms of its ability to generate income. The economy is seen by politicians and experts of all stripes as the sole reasonable indicator of societal and individual prosperity.

This instrumentalization of man and environment as commerce items or services is reassuring to decision-makers, but it severely impoverishes reality. And it has this inertia power of loose ideas, which enables it to apply its universalistic conclusions to every new occurrence. Thus, critical sentiments regarding multinational corporations, petitions from impoverished nations asking a fair price for agricultural commodities, and the Rio summit debate were absorbed. Curiously, if the topic is not discussed by the governing circles themselves, economic dialogue does not exist. Therefore, the rare rational critique of the origins of drug trafficking is masked by the enormous demand in the North and the profitability of crops in the South. Consequently, the globalization of mass information networks progresses without highlighting its financial structures and power dynamics.

Everything fits, and everything is destroyed with care since everything depends on the objectification of humans. All people with the ability to disseminate ideas are obligated to inform all other human components. Thus, the fate of the Haitian people would become *economic* hominies! And who is more dependent on the economy of its neighbors?

2.2.2 Imposed structural adjustment

The structural adjustment recommended by foreign donors and provided to governments seeking loans or grants for the development of their individual countries attempts to clean up the conditions for receiving help and realign the key financial and economic balances in these nations.

- Balance of exports and imports in terms of money
- Government downsizing and reductions in public spending
- Devaluation of the country's currency
- Restructuring or selling of government-owned businesses
- Elimination of administrative and quota constraints throughout time

This is a set of measures, especially monetary, called technical. All this to guarantee the repayment of loans.[14]

However, there is risk. If these actions are reasonable (and who, in reality, could contest the concept of realism in the administration of public finances?), then they come after decades of laissez-faire and even incentives provided by wealthy nations to borrowing nations to assume complete responsibility for development of finance. Consequently, these affluent nations have become the major employers of underdeveloped nations, which are also lousy leaders. Large populations of formerly rural people have seen their way of life become unstable and their methods of produc-

---

[14] Deshommes, Fritz. Néo-Libéralisme, Crise Economique et Alternative de Développement. Presses de l'Imprimeur II (1995): 18–19.

tion vanish. Also, do these measures arrive too late and do they frequently miss their intended target? According to IMF analysts, program implementation is frequently followed with an increase in prices and a decline in growth rates.

The impact of the sanctions imposed on the solicitor countries are felt in three ways: by undermining their sovereignty, by inflicting more misery on their citizens, and by destabilizing their governments. In the developing world, social peace, social justice, and freedom are therefore threatened in the name of the economic dogmatism of the great powers, as applied directly through their bilateral cooperation or through development assistance institutions such as the International Monetary Fund or, closer to Haiti, the Inter-American Development Bank (IDB). The failings of development policy based on an ideology bloc (monetarist neoliberalism) have eroded the legitimacy of authority and the borrowing countries almost everywhere in any sense. What George Corn referred to as the "new global economic chaos."

2.2.3 Effects of structural adjustment on Haitian agriculture

What transpired and what were the results of structural adjustment in Haiti? At the end of the reign of Duvalier II (who was president of Haiti from 1971 to 1986), the new ethic of the government appeared to be affirmed through new fiscal measures such as the tax application on income, new control procedures on public expenditure and public enterprises, the elimination of tax privileges, and the restructuring of public companies or even the closing of those with poor performance.

The removal of differentiated tariffs for imported goods, the decline in the general level of external protection, and the application of internal taxes on commodities promote lower prices and microcommerce but have two perverse dramatic effects: unfair competition made by importations (particularly through smuggling) on Haitian agricultural products (rice from Artibonite, for example) and the rise of narcotraffic in the wake of deregulation.[15]

In 1990, the Haitian currency is no longer subsidized

---

[15] "According to Economist Fritz Deshommes, this is a palliative to the idea that agriculture should be oriented toward the production of fruit and vegetables exports like coffee, cocoa, and wood commercial."

and reverts to its true values relative to the US dollar. Lastly, if small urban consumers' purchasing power momentarily increased at the time of Jean-Claude Duvalier's overthrow, the ensuing sharp increase in prices afterward diminished it.

As a result of globalization, farmers have problems selling their produce. The government, which is likewise in a state of distress, permits all types of competition and is unable to combat the increase in economic crime. In addition, the embargo imposed after the military coup in 1991 has worsened Haiti's economic and health decline.

In addition, the administration that emerged from the elections of 1991 had provided nothing better. Its instructions were not encouraging, and its duration was insufficient. The coup that ensued distorted any objective evaluation of Aristide-Préval's government.

However, it is important to emphasize a little-known component of the Aristide-Préval administration prior to September 30, 1991. Completing the restoration and effectiveness program of previous Haitian administrations, the then-Executive formulated an economic policy centered on bolstering the agriculture sector.

In July 1991, they reached an unprecedented agreement with all foreign assistance donors for a $450 million investment package spanning three to five years. The coup d'état and ensuing embargo placed on Haiti by the international community at Aristide's request prevented the program's execution. Rather, it had expedited the utter poverty of the masses, the devastation of the middle classes, siphoning, and the abandonment of a nation with economic, environmental, social, health, and political problems.

If the conditionality of development aid played a significant part in the demise of the dictatorship in Haiti, it is regrettable that foreign powers previously supported and accommodated it. They have also, if too slowly, backed the apparent new democratic government that has been in the process of becoming and has been delegitimized by the coup, resulting in the immediate suspension of aid, but to no use. It appears that the policy of development aid is a tough weapon to wield for both donors and receivers, reflecting the complexities of the interstate system.

Lastly and primarily in the current climate, what strategy should be adopted for Haiti, if not the distinctive and authentic politics of the farmland?

The Haitian industrialist Louis Déjoie put it eloquently in the following terms: "And the farmland, after all, has meaning only in terms of human relations, that depending on the lives of men who occupy and exploit it. If it no longer fulfills its role to ensure a decent life for men who cultivate it, it becomes an urgent need for government agencies to ensure that our laws, instead of expressing abusive relationships between the city and the country-side, between the peasantry and the rural and urban bourgeoisie, express correct relations between the entire community and the country's productive resources."[16]

---

[16] Lespès, Anthony. *Journal La Nation*, no. 485. Juillet 11, 1946.

PART 2

Agricultural Sector in Regard of Law, Habits, and Customs of Haitian Peasant

C H A P T E R 3

IMPACTS OF SUCCESSION LAW ON AGRICULTURE

Section 1: Human and economic importance

1.1 Predominance of system grapillage

The agricultural sector is important to developing nations, particularly for countries like Haiti that are—after so many years—still in the first stages of development.

Agriculture (crops and animals) employs over 70 percent of the working population compared to 3 percent in the United States and 6 percent in France. In recent years, the traditional mode of production known as gleaning has regained prominence in Haiti; derived from places to live in colonial period and in the early years after independence, it has been reinforced by the marginalization and social isolation of the peasantry and the absence of innovation and capitalization among small farm holders. Even in the setting of significant agriculture (sugarcane), the working process and performance are low, and rural communities profit little from the very uneven distribution of revenue.

Another characteristic is the significance of soil as a production factor: the soil's quality, location (plain, dull), precipitation, and climate, in general, are among the numerous factors that govern the use of agricultural land and the technical and production methods employed. If soil is a natural resource, its distribution, usage, and even its production are far more influenced by social interactions.

Finally, it is agriculture alone that ultimately produces food (and other commodities) for the entire society. Therefore, it plays a crucial role in the distribution of wealth, social equilibrium in autonomy, national dependency, and economics. It is virtually completely reliant on the land

and labor of the land that modern Haiti's development is too low and too uneven.

1.2. General features of the Haitian farmer family

Anthropologists who have examined the Black family structure in the New World, particularly in the Caribbean, highlight two key aspects: the significance of the household, which is the basic functional unit, comes first, then the matrifocality of the family, that is, the requisite existence of one or more matri-nuclear cells with numerous polygamous arrangement options.

The home is described as a collection of humans residing under the same roof, participating in almost identical activities and relying on the same resources for subsistence. It provides surveillance, biological reproduction, cultural, educational, social, and religious transmission, economic assistance, and social identification for its members. Due to the ambiguous and evasive nature of man's position and his irresponsible behavior, his progeniture, the home has assumed a matrifocal form. Rarely does the desired young woman get independence from her mother's home. Even if it means isolating her own residence, she will always do it in looking for her mother's protection in any circumstances. Moreover, the status of parent, spouse, or partner is typically associated by obvious absenteeism and a minimal economic involvement. This mindset exacerbates the mother's role and domestic responsibilities at home.

These characteristics apply to Haitian society. The home described by anthropologists resembles our idea of "community household" in that it is a form of extended family in which everyone lives under the authority of the family head. Also included in the community household are godparents, godchildren, grandparents, and *collaterals*.[17]

---

[17] It is a lineage system where rights on land materialize belonging to a kind of society of parents for which land, representing the concrete element of social cohesion, is, by definition, inalienable.

However, matrifocality is difficult to discuss in the traditional rural *plaçage*—free union—which is like a stable marriage. The family unit is physically separated from the husband's parents, and the nuclearization of the property around the father and mother demonstrates the father's leadership, presence, and economic activities. A specific distribution of work strengthens parental group's ties of unity and continuity. It is a straightforward sociological justification for polygamy. Family features that transcend the conventional relationship to a nuclear social unit.

In rural areas, a "free union" is really a stable, consensual relationship that carries responsibilities and obligations codified by customary law. In this instance, the guy has a number of women, including an upright lady (a matron), who is the most significant, and other women often referred to as outside women or kenge.

Sometimes, economic and societal imperatives influence this decision. The fragmentation of landownership and the vast distance between different parcels of land forces the farmer to distribute operational positions for the utilization of his property. Installation of a family satisfies the requirement for economic order and simplifies business interactions. Socially, plate or free union in rural areas expands the familial circle and satisfies the desire for communication and communal life.

Everyone is aware that 90 percent of the rural population is involved in agriculture, yet this fact does not come without significant disadvantages. Despite the legislator's good intentions, the rural environment's succession *law*,[18] filiation, marriage regime, customs, and traditions might be the clear source of massive land conflicts with detrimental consequences on soil exploitation. Thus, disputes and excessive fragmentation of land are prevalent in rural areas of Haiti. In certain

---

[18] System of property, or the individual subject of right, *su juris*, and the land has become an exchange value. In this system, formalized by the Civil Code, "no one is bound to remain in joint ownership."

instances, it leads in brutal conflicts that cause enormous human and economic costs.

Section 2: Succession law and Haitian peasant

2.1. The right of succession

2.1.1 Definition

An estate or succession is the legal transfer of a deceased person's assets and obligations to surviving individuals. The law differentiates between succession right, succession order, testamentary succession, and ab intestato succession.

The right of succession is the most tangible result of kinship, blood link, but not exclusively as it also affects nonrelative spouses. The inheritance of the deceased is distributed in a certain sequence and proportion to the deceased's parents and spouse. This can only be explained if we consider that the kinfolk or the household possessed virtual coproperty rights over this inheritance. The concept of familial ownership historically underpins the right of succession.

According to this theory, the succession is contingent upon the presumed distribution of the deceased's estate. By selecting parents that succeed upon death, the law makes it such that legal succession of the deceased's property does not let the presents that the deceased may have received to be separated from family rights.

2.1.2 Estates ab intestacy

First, it is essential to establish which family members are designated to inherit the "person's estate that it is" (equals *de cujus successione agitus*) or "de cujus" as it is usually known.

Then it must be determined how that which was a vocation, anticipation, or acquired right becomes a reality and how inherited vocations are carried out upon the death of the "de cujus." The death which inaugurates the succession.

2.1.2.1 Succession by vocations

They are governed by the law. The legislation specifies to whom the estate will be addressed and transferred. One can separate a devolution principle and extraordinary devolutions.

The devolution concept applies to blood relationships, whether lawful or natural, without the intervention of a living spouse or, very rarely, an adulterous child. While the exception that produces the unusual devolution may be due to a variety of factors, such as the presence of a living spouse or an illegitimate child, the lack of any family may also be a factor (devolution to the state through its government). In fact, the devolution principle comprises statistically more than half of all cases, as it affects the estate of the last surviving spouse in every family, in addition to the succession of single and divorced individuals.

2.1.2.2 The devolution principle

As a corollary to the principle of equality, there is no distinction between legitimate and natural filiation (reservation made, however, of the illegitimate child) or legitimate heirs are classified into four groups or orders based on their relationship to the dead. Within each sequence, it must prioritize according to the nearest degree but only within each order; for instance, a grandchild, parent of second degree, has precedence over a father, parent of first degree, because they belong to separate orders.

2.1.2.2.1 The descending order

The descendants are referred to as the first line. The closest heirs in degree exclude the farthest heirs (son succeeds to the exclusion of grandson). However, representation is necessary in some situations; if the dead had many children, the deceased's grandson will inherit in place of their deceased father or mother. They get just the portion of their grandparent's inheritance that their deceased parent would have received in competition with uncles and aunts who are sons and daughters of the deceased but more closely related to them.

The descendants get equal inheritances. This is the notion of equality between siblings which has political resonance. It comprises the eradication of primogeniture and the male advantage that existed in the ancient feudal legislation prior to 1789. However, the father retains the option of allocating a bigger portion to one of his children to preserve the family's wealth, giving or bequeathing to the kid (who may or may not be the eldest) the available share, the share of assets that it may have without depleting the reserve.

2.1.2.2.2 The hierarchy of favored ascendants and collaterals

By absence of descendants, the law establishes a composite order including, on one side, the decedent's parents and, on the other, his siblings and descendants of siblings (nieces and nephews).

How will the estate be divided between them?

If the dead leaves his father, mother, and privileged collaterals concurrently, the father receives a quarter of the estate, the mother receives a quarter, and the remaining half is divided evenly (considering, wherever feasible, the proper representation) among the privileged collaterals.

However, there may be brothers or half brothers among them. Then, the notion of the slot comes into action, which entails separating the estate into two sections, one of which is reserved for privileged collaterals.

Siblings (brothers and sisters from the same father and mother) will participate in both lines; however, consanguineous and uterine relationships will only be represented in one line (so that the part of the brothers is twice that of half brothers).

If the dead left a parent on one hand and privileged collaterals on the other, the ascending survivor receives a quarter of the estate, and the remaining three quarters are split among the privileged collaterals.

If the dead left neither parent but just privileged collaterals, only the collaterals will inherit. In contrast, if the dead left just his father and mother and no favored collaterals, the father and mother will get equal shares of the whole inheritance. If the dead has left neither parent without privileged collaterals, the parent inherits the entire inheritance even if the other line has regular collaterals. Thus, maternal or paternal uncles or cousins cannot seek, based on the slot, a portion of the inheritance with the surviving father. However, if the dead also left a surviving spouse, she/he can play the slot for her/his own advantage and shares with the father or mother; the other half should have been distributed to favored collaterals on the maternal or paternal side.

2.1.2.2.3 The ordinary ascendants' order

All ascendants other than the deceased's father and mother, including grandparents, great-grandparents, etc., are called by using the slot concept between them but without representation. The closest one in each of the maternal and paternal lineages eliminates the farthest one.

They are summoned by the absence of the deceased's father, mother, and favored collaterals. However, it is possible that the dead leaves behind a privileged ascendant in one line and a common ascendant in the other (example: his father and maternal grandfather). Using the slot concept, the estate is then split into two equal parts: one-half goes to the ascendant (preferred or ordinary) of each line.

The ordinary ascendant excludes all ordinary collaterals, even those of the line to which he does not belong. He may, however, have a favored ascendant divide the inheritance equally with the surviving spouse under the same terms.

2.1.2.2.4 The ordinary collateral's order

These are all the collaterals besides the privileged collaterals: practically, uncles, aunts, cousins, etc. However, they are not summoned indefinitely. They succeed to the sixth degree inclusively (cousins come from Germans). Exceptionally, however, they are called up to the twelfth degree when the dead was unable to create a will during his final years due to insanity. It is thought that if he had been able to, he would have contacted his/her estate's collateral from far and diverse lines.

The existence of an ordinary ascendant in either of the two lines is sufficient to separate the usual collaterals; for instance, paternal cousins cannot claim anything when a maternal grandmother is present.

When there are typical collaterals in both the paternal and maternal lines, the slot principle must first be applied between them. Then, in each line, the degree closest eliminates the degree farthest away. If one of the two lines has no collaterals to the degree of succession, those of the other lines take all (interlinear devolution).

2.1.2.3 The exceptional devolution
2.1.2.3.1 The surviving spouse

It is only the ally (in the broad sense, distinct from the blood tie) that is expected to succeed. Her vocation is sometimes residual (due to the lack of a blood tie) and sometimes concurrent (in competition with parents). The residual vocation is practiced in full ownership, but the concurrent vocation is only applicable in usufruct so that the family's capital is kept by blood.

The survivor's inheritance rights are still contingent on the existence of the marriage tie. Divorce causes them to fall even about an innocent partner. Separation of spouse or separation of body preserves the legal distinctions between them.

2.1.2.3.2 Adulterine child

As long as it does not conflict with the marriage against which adultery was done so that it does not compete with the surviving spouse and the legitimate offspring of the harmed union, it is a natural child like all the others. If he is acknowledged by his father who is in the marriage, he is illegitimate. In essence, he does not inherit as it is acknowledged that "bastards do not inherit"; yet he is entitled to financial assistance until he reaches adulthood. However, his parents may assign in advance, by way of a gift, the equivalent of his hereditary portion to avoid the spouse and legitimate children from a potentially morally difficult legal encounter. However, if the adulterous parent leaves no successor, he can claim the entire fortune, at least in some nations after significant legal controversy.

2.1.2.3.3 The state

The *state* collects the whole inheritance in the absence of succeeding parents and a living spouse. Moreover, in all estates left in inheritance (particularly in France), the state seizes inheritance rights, which amounts to a capital tax.

2.2 The opening of succession

It occurs by death a devolution of the estate as inheritance, devolution of legacy, which is a collection of assets and liabilities; the successor inherits the property but is also liable for debts; it is a successor in universal title.

By virtue of a person's passing, he acquires ownership of the property he inherits, regardless of the role he ultimately plays in the succession. The legitimate and natural heirs, as well as the surviving spouse, are instantly seized of the rights and acts of the deceased, allowing them to exercise their succession rights on the estate. This is referred to as the referral, the authority to move instantly, without formality or oversight, into possession of the estate: the authority to exercise all rights related to the ship's heirship.

In contrast, the trial court should grant possession to the state. Its inheritance rights depend on the lack of preferred heirs and must thus be legally validated. This appears to be a form of familial privilege; it represents a notion of familial co-ownership.

2.3 The liberalities

Donations or provisions as free gifts are judicial acts designed to deliver an economic benefit to an individual without regard, a totally gratuitous benefit. Contrary to the concept of familial ownership and conservation of possessions in the family—which has been so strong in the ancient law and which the contemporary law, despite its individuality, does not fully disregard—the law has always exhibited an attitude of mistrust toward presents. Unquestionably, presents may be used to favor one parent or kid over the others. However, it is then the spirit of equality resulting from the revolution that is wounded.

As part of our theme, we could only address succession law and charity in the bare minimum detail required to depict the family as a legal entity.

2.4 Succession and successible degree in rural area

As can be observed, the civil code grants precedence and exclusivity to acknowledged children, followed by favored collaterals, siblings, sisters, nephews, and ascendants; in the absence of all these individuals, uncles, cousins whose vocation extends to the sixth degree. To refer to an informal level, the type of succession in rural areas deviates seamlessly from the adverse matter of recognition inflamed by the civil code and installs all offspring, whether they have been recognized or not, under a universal title. In addition, in rural places, custom creates a favorable circumstance for the eldest son, and according to Dr. Romain, the eldest inherited the farm's primary residence. The bequest also contains the most magnificent garden since the eldest son frequently assisted his father throughout planting and harvesting seasons. The oldest finally obtains the inheritance of his sisters who reside under the same roof as him. He must mature for the sake of his sisters. The dead is expected to transfer his rights and patriarchal privileges to the eldest son. The oldest becomes a type of executor of the will.

In this situation, the peasant, outside the legal system, has given himself a tool to manage succession without being able to remove the potential of disagreement among heirs, particularly when the court must rule based on positive law.

2.5 Consequences on agriculture

Should we note in this context the various land gifts and donations made by the leadership in the first years after independence, particularly by the emperor Jean-Jacques Dessalines, Alexandre Pétion, Jean-Pierre Boyer, and until the revolution of 1843 led by Jean-Jacques Acaau? We would be confronted with the configuration of interminable conflicts that persist and prevail even today in our country and, more specifically, especially in the Artibonite valley. Likewise, our investigations[19] indicate, among other things, the following:

- Social conduct such as excessive concubine use, monetary regimes, the generous effects of sex outside marriage, legitimate descent, natural descent, and the legal circumstances for natural offspring, kinship, and marriage further complicate an already complex scenario.

---

[19] Moral, Paul. *Le Paysan Haïtien*, pp. 180–182.

- The rural home in the Haitian society was effectively governed by customary law. How might it be conceivable, even under customary law, to clear such a complicated situation involving countless descendants from all origins and directions?

- The plating or free union is the most sustainable type of familial life. The sheer nature of this hierarchy is that the children of the first receive their birth certificates more readily. However, parental authority is supreme in this subject, and the kid will only be registered if the father consents. Only if the guy rejects paternity is the burden of registration transferred on the female.

- Godparents exercise a significant impact on the kid. Once appointed, they can intervene personally to expedite the child's record (their godson). In the majority of rural areas, the gossip or godfather holds the birth certificate until the child reaches majority. He is entitled to this privilege because the baptism incurred expenses. Godparents are potential substitutes for absent, incapacitated, or deceased parents.

- The birth of a child outside of a hospital offers significant obstacles to its registration. Even when the farmer eventually arrives in town to obtain the birth certificate, it contains names that severely impede the newborn's registration. Adopting a surname from one generation to the next gives rise to chaos. On his marriage, the farmer changes his name to emphasize his possession of a piece of land. He claims his father's, grandfather's, and great-grandfather's names. Adopting a nickname frequently complicates the individual. For instance, Pierre Duplan Bulidor gives birth to Pierrismé Pierre and Pierre Philistine in the valley of Artibonite. Joseph Etienne is the son of Etienne Pierre, who, in turn, is the grandson of Pierre-Paul Rival. Some personal names also allude to reference groups, such as soldiers, state leaders, priests, etc.

In brief, it is a mostly rural society in which most of the population is engaged in agricultural activities in tiny settlements that lack even the most elementary forms of civilization. Among these individuals, social issues are particularly severe. In contrast to metropolitan regions, the countryside is served by a negligible number of social, administrative, professional, educational, and environmental technicians and service providers. The inability to strictly regulate births and deaths paralyzes accurate knowledge of population movements across the country.

In addition to this unfortunate circumstance, the few governmental administrations that service the rural populace are frequently under-resourced and controlled in most cases by incompetent and dishonest agents. This reality can only exacerbate family conflicts in rural areas and endanger the exploitation of disputed land. In addition, the occurrences are assuming progressively colossal dimensions across the nation, which may partially account for the reduction in agricultural output.

CHAPTER 4

PERSPECTIVE OF AGRICULTURAL REGULATIONS IN HAITI

Haiti is entitled to develop independently its own trajectory. In agriculture, the current technique resembles the community approach. This strategy, which has been implemented in all rural sectors, merits additional examination. We must proceed by requesting legislation directly related to the exploitation of Haitian agricultural space, at the intersection or not of public and private initiatives for development, while focusing on the subsequent constraints to gain a clear understanding on the scope of path to take.

Section 1: Legal provisions linked to agricultural area

1.1 Agriculture seen by the Haitian legislator from 1826–1889

By the repeal of the Rural Code of May 6, 1826, in 1843, all succeeding Haitian governments—regardless of their ideology, philosophy, and policy—realized that the country's economy and wealth relied on the growth of agriculture. Additionally, everyone had attempted to encourage and defend the sector in an effective manner. All had attempted to replace the legislation of 1826 with a better one, but it is also true that all efforts and endeavors had had nearly negative outcomes.

The law of August 16, 1862, signed by President Geffrard, was supposed to replace the previous laws and protect the country's land security through solid legislation. However, it was subsequently shown to be difficult to implement and incapable of producing the necessary results.

The law of August 16, 1862, was superseded by the statute of October 10, 1863, in less than a year. This legislation, which repealed only that of August 16, 1862, permitted the executive branch to take by decree the steps essential for good rural police subject to congressional approval.

A report addressed to the president of Haiti by the Interior and Agriculture Secretary of State at the end of December 1863 and published in the *Monitor* on January 2, 1864, revealed that under this authority, the Rural Code in effect at the time was reviewed and prepared in the form of an executive order; the decree was then published in the official journal (numbers 6 and 7) in January 1864.

The same report also detailed the phases through which this project had traveled. First presented to the Council of Secretaries of State where it underwent an initial examination, then submitted to a commission composed of competent and enlightened men in which it was carefully examined, then forwarded to all commanders of the districts who were invited to give their opinion after consulting with local committees to review the draft. This project returned a second time before the Council of Secretaries of State, which, after many meetings, reevaluated articles and revisions offered by regional commissions. Then it was determined that the proposal would be transformed into a bill and submitted to the legislature for approval.

The law was eventually enacted by the Senate on October 18, 1864, and by the House of Representatives on October 24, 1864, and proclaimed by the Executive branch on October 27, 1864, following lengthy and illuminating debates.

It should be noted that the Rural Code of 1825, which was enacted earlier to the ordinance of October 27, 1864, was influenced by the beliefs of the period. Many of its chapters, particularly those pertaining to contracts and agreements between owners, farmers, and growers, were motivated by an overzealous desire to regulate everything, were tainted with arbitrariness and favoritism, and were detrimental to the principles of individual liberty and private transactions. This code, which was also excellent in its other provisions on the protection of property and labor, people's safety, and general rural police, was subjected to partial attacks upon its publication and then to a near-unanimous and systematic opposition so that, without being repealed, it fell out of use.

In 1836, the House of Representatives addressed the repeal in the following words in its historic response to President Boyer's inaugural session address:

> The Rural Code was repealed, and its repeal devastated agriculture. But it must be acknowledged that it suffered the fate of all institutions that are not in the spirit of a century of progress…bereft of the sanction of public opinion, the interest itself was unable to ensure its early extinction. We think, however, that we may proceed without fear of controversy, that the code, once changed and adapted to the demands of the current day, will create the most positive results.

Governments that succeeded President Boyer had forgotten the chamber of 1836's last counsel, which was so sagely advised. One might recall the reform supported by the presidency of Lysius Félicité Salomon Jeune in 1883; this reform was inspired by the idea of the late Dr. Louis-Joseph Janvier, who was attracted by the agrarian policy pursued by the American administration at that time. The Haitian strategy consisting of the distribution of no more than twenty acres of land to peasants failed because it was unable to give the tools to guide the then-bourgeoisie through an industrial policy that supported small-scale agricultural exploitation.

1.2 Agriculture seen by the Haitian legislator from 1934–1986

From 1934, the Haitian legislature expressed its desire to shape the rural community in its most ideal form. The provisions of the legislation of Rural Family Property approved by the Haitian

Congress on January 1, 1934, are highly visible. Below are the essential parts of Rural Family Property bill:

- *Article 1.* Any portion of the private domain of the State that is appropriate for farming and does not exceed twenty acres shall be made available to any Haitian who qualifies under the criteria of this legislation and has fulfilled the procedures outlined in an illusive parcel of land known as rural property of family. It is not possible to create more than one rural property of family for the same individual.
- *Article 2.* Conditions Under Obtention of Rural Property of Family.

    Any Haitian of at least twenty-one years of age, of either sex, may acquire a suitable rural family property from available government private land, provided:

- ✓ he has rented a farm from the government for a minimum of two years;
- ✓ he notifies the General Administration of Taxation on a form created for that purpose of his desire to become a holder of a rural family property;
- ✓ at the request of possession of needed land, he has resided in the field for two years prior to receiving the title under the Rural Family Property Act;
- ✓ he has consistently paid all annual fees; and
- ✓ he has kept the land in good condition and has been farming according to the certificate signed by an agent of the National Service for

Agricultural Production
and Rural Education.

Under concussion reserve, the certificate required by this statute is granted at no cost. Less
than a year later, on September
4, 1934, this legislation was
revised by an amendment say-
ing that government farmers
who have inhabited a rural
property for ten years and who
have paid their non-prescrip-
tion-related expenses consistently throughout these ten
years may acquire these rural
properties quickly with respect
to the provisions of this law.
In accordance with articles 5 and
6 of the law of January 12,
1934, they shall receive their
final and irreversible title if the
director general of taxes issues
a positive report and the following requirements are met:

- ✓ They provide notification on a form provided for that purpose by the General Administration of Taxation of their plan to become a holder of a rural family property.
- ✓ They have personally dwelt on the property for ten years and increased its worth at their own expense and without subleasing.
- ✓ All annual fees are paid on a consistent basis.
- ✓ They have kept the parcel of land in excellent condition and have been farming according to the certificate signed by an agent of the National Service for Agricultural Production and Rural Education, as amended by the statute

of September 4, 1934 (*Moniteur*, 1939, no. 82).

It should be noted that the provisions of September 21, 1939, bill will be redefined and reinforced by two subsequent laws:

➢ The legislation of September 15, 1939, on concession given to settlers as Rural Family Property regarding parcels of land to which they are or will be properly linked for at least one year (*Moniteur*, 1939, no. 77).

➢ The legislation of September 8, 1948, stating that every individual owning as a farmer a piece of land from the government's private domain in the cities of thirty, forty, fifty, and sixty classes and neigh-borhoods, if he has worked it for at least five years (now twenty years) and owns a construction/*national gift*.[20] Here are some provisions from this statute:

- *Article 9.* A portion of this legislation will be posted on rental and lease application forms for land from the private domain of the government in designated localities.
- *Article 10.* Titles of National Donation shall be awarded by the President of the Republic of

---

[20] *Moniteur*, no. 100. October 28, 1948.

Haiti to each beneficiary of this law. Before their distribution, these titles will be numbered and recorded in a special register maintained by the General Direction of Contributions. In addition, they will be documented and transcribed as required by law for registration and hypothec to the vigilance of the administration.

- *Article 11.* The national gift is indivisible and inalienable. It can only be transferred by inheritance.

The decree creating a special court in the plain of Artibonite on November 23, 1950:

- *Article 1.* For the cadastral district of the plain of Artibonite, a special tribunal with headquarters in Saint-Marc with full jurisdiction over the whole region mentioned in the first item of the March 17, 1950, order is established. This court is known as the "Land Court" of the Plaine de l'Artibonite.

- *Article 2.* All contests, disputes, and litigation emerging in the current cadastral district, irrespective of the type of the possessory or *pétitoire*, shall be submitted before the special court, which shall have exclusive jurisdiction over all other regular courts. This court will know, among other things, actions directly linked to Development

Organism of the Artibonite Valley, institution acting on behalf of the government for the creation of cadastre through the territorial area described by the decree of March 17, 1950, which border actions of all those relating to the establishment or recognition of property rights on land to be registered, the related acquisitive requirements, questions of mental, capacity, or identity, and actions relating to the establishment or recognition of property rights.

- *Article 3.* In instances directly involving the Artibonite Development Agency, the director of cadastral registry will represent the government in cadastral activities of the district and will seize by simple request the "Land Court."

The law of August 13, 1951, strengthened the decree of November 23, 1950, in its articles 4–6:

- *Article 4.* In the event of a disagreement impeding the ultimate delimitation of a land parcel, the rules of article 8, paragraph 2, of the decree of August 18, 1950, on the cadastre of the plain of Artibonite must apply.
- *Article 5.* The party that will oppose the final delimitation of a piece of land shall—within three days, the time limit specified in article 8, paragraph 2, of the decree of August 18, 1950, on the cadastre of the plain Artibonite—seize by summons the special court of his opposition for a final decision.
- *Article 6.* Failing to do so, the government commissioner (the district's government attorney) to the court, based on a mem-

ory from the cadastral office of the plain of Artibonite containing the names of the parties, the date of the opposition, and the location of the piece of land in dispute, will call by the citation given at the request of the Haitian government and served personally or at home for the trial of the cause in three days for any reprieve besides that of distance.

The decree of October 18, 1961, on "Land Court" creating a specific method for producing Artibonite[21] valley maps quickly.

The decree of March 4, 1974, pertaining to the Agrarian Commission:[22]

- *Article 1.* The Presidential Permanent Agrarian Commission is a consultative body tasked with providing advice on agrarian

---

[21] *Moniteur*, no. 100. October 28, 1948.
[22] Ibid.

issues such as the distribution of land to peasants, the transfer of ownership to government farmers, the establishment of farm workers on unoccupied government land, and large-scale leasing contracts. It is an executive commission with the authority to investigate rural evictions to restore the victim's right to enjoy his property. It has the authority to intervene when the event occurs on undeveloped territory in the suburbs of the capital and other cities of the republic.

- *Article 2.* Dispossession is the consequence of force, misuse of authority, or deception. Any physical deprivation or fear of dispossession may be the basis of a complaint to the commission.

Section 2: Causes and failures of past experiences

2.1 Constraints of Political, Social,
and Cultural Order

Considering the abovementioned laws, decrees, and directives, the Haitian parliament has always desired to maintain the sustainability of Haiti's arable land to increase agricultural production through direct management of government and private farms. Nevertheless, the accompanying figures pertaining to exported items indicate a downturn in Haitian agriculture. Consequently, both agricultural production and exports of agricultural products continue to decline. This had adverse effects on the nation and rural communities. It appears that the legal method, as it is currently defined, faces several political, social, and cultural obstacles that may in many situations prove to be sources of land conflicts in the nation, especially in the Artibonite region:

- In the Haitian peasants, land purchase is conducted without legal procedures under the auspices of good neighborliness between the seller and the buyer. This is an exception to the idea that "title verifies the right in real estate affairs."

- There is frequent political involvement in judicial decisions. In most land-related litigation cases, judges are required to follow the directives of high-ranking government officials, regardless of the legal framework. Despite their repeated assertions, there are plaintiffs whose original titles have been taken from them. And victims remain silent until the appropriate moment to carry out violent acts to reclaim their property. This leads in violent fights, and none of the combatants can improve the area in question.
- Problems associated with illiteracy in rural regions cause peasants to disregard the law by doing

criminal activities that may be coherent with their thinking but are penalized by law according to the adage "Everyone is assumed to know the law." Nonetheless, does customary law not adhere to the continual majority opinion? In contrast, in Haiti, a country with a rising illiteracy rate, the tradition frequently conflicts with the law, which considers it a criminal or civil crime or both. This dilemma confronts, for instance, the Haitian farmer who unintentionally becomes the cause of his own damnation through succession. Thus, the peasant is exposed to the law, and his only recourse is to turn to faulty practices that threaten the productivity of the inherited property, regardless of what could happen to the land when the estate is opened at the owner's death.

- Numerous heirs to a tiny parcel of property.
- Multiple individuals having seemingly valid legal documents for the same piece of land.

All this legislation has a fatal flaw: the associated measures are not considered, and even when they are, monitoring is not assured. The decadal prescription for unoccupied land is, in fact, a measure of protection for farmers without title: in practice, most of these farmers, unable to afford the costs of a trial, are sometimes obliged to surrender their plots legitimately earned through use and time in favor of distant owners. The Wedesbrandt case in the lagoon of Lachicotte (February 1952) is a superb example of this circumstance; this case has brought to light the mismatch between customs. And the agricultural land suffers because of peasant marginalization and death. This may be summarized as follows:

- ✓ Government efforts aimed at assisting farmers in rural regions are made occasionally and planned with insufficient professional rigor or inadequate technology. In other terms, long-term and often even shorter-term maintenance of the farmer's uncommon agricultural equipment and infrastructure is not guaranteed.

- ✓ The socio-environmental economics of the peasant are extremely restricted; they tend to stifle any development made by a group not imposed by force. There is no national development dynamic that would solidify any improvement by attracting people who have not yet benefited rather than separating those who are already gaining expertise.

- ✓ The local and technical competence, as well as the technical culture of the community as a whole, are insufficient to avoid the deterioration of works over time.

✓ There is insufficient convergence between private and public interests since the domains of individual and collective property ownership are not clearly defined in any project's surroundings (although they are well-defined in the project activity itself).

✓ The uncertainty of the socio-economic environment, pricing, smuggling, transportation, inefficient government policies, and repression invalidate all activity and profit projections.

✓ Everything is interconnected and a priority, and, first, it is extremely difficult for Haitian peasants to make a livelihood, send their children to school, and construct a future under these conditions.

✓ The duration of the initiatives is insufficient, and it is not anticipated that they will last.

Once, Paul Moral posed the question "Would the strength of tradition, the solidarity of the community, and the legal provisions themselves be sufficient to defend farmers from powerful and organized appetites?"

In other words, what option exists to safeguard the peasant? And what tool will serve as a socio-legal trigger for a better agricultural organization in rural Haiti? Is there no need to consider a reform of the past?

2.2 Agro-land reform

We must discuss an agricultural ownership reform in Haiti. It is one of the legal components of fundamental reforms that impact Haiti's growth. Recent research has demonstrated that it has not been a battle for land between the bourgeoisie and the peasantry. Rather, the social issue was the control of the market for agricultural products. The Caribbean peasantries—and the Haitian peasantry was a pioneer in this regard—managed the land, their space, and their production themselves. On the other hand, there is a clear conflict between the equality of inheritance distribution and its inherent imprescriptibly and the strategies adopted by farmers to handle population pressure and low productivity. The agricultural history of Haiti adequately justifies the importance of small property and small commodity family farms in agrarian transformation. Therefore, Haiti needs a land strategy that prioritizes the long-term viability of agriculture.

This reform will be founded on the idea of land development; it will stimulate the reorganization of fragmented parcels around residential areas; it will promote direct faire-valoir; it will discourage absentee landlords; and it will replace customary law with more formal regulations. Consistent with municipal duty, it will enable the equitable and just resolution of land security issues in rural areas. This audacious policy might be implemented and carried out without causing societal anguish, but it will require the engagement of social actors, local authorities, and the rule of law. It also necessitates the execution of the decentralization envisioned by the constitution of 1987 and legal and economic changes that would enable Haiti's institutions to marry the objectives that will be assigned to the country.

These initiatives should be accompanied by a sustained national effort to boost agricultural production, focusing on the training and mentoring of farmers. In this setting and because of the fulfillment of these requirements, the Haitian peasants will progressively reap the rewards of their work and investments; and as a result, they will modernize and increase their outputs. Haiti will require the engagement of everyone: farmers, agronomists, attorneys, local representatives, municipalities, government officials, entrepreneurs, investors and bankers, merchants and craftsmen, nongovernmental organizations, collaboration, and foreign help. Here are the components of a new economic policy proposal designed by specialists in rural development. What vector will it employ? Public discourse and/or community action?

2.3 Speech and community action
2.3.1 Definition of elements

Well-integrated into the surroundings, community action promotes innovations and makes service and new equipment accessible to everybody with its public service purpose prominently evident. Avoiding the political discourse, community speech actually prepares *Republican political word*—secularism (e.g., freedom of religion, universality toward achieved results within the previously defined community framework, participation to the construction and maintenance works that familiarize excluded people with concepts of citizenship duties, training in collective management of public facilities, equality of principle of speech, and first reflections on conflicts between public services and private interests).

Community is action or else it is ineffective. It is never restricted to speech and prayer. It enrolls quickly in embodiments. It battles reality, seeks efficiency, and is willing to compromise if necessary. It always encounters a dearth of resources, yet it always finds answers. So, upon deeper inspection, there is pooling of resources on projects according to the extant structures of the community, which would be updated to reflect one another's interests.

2.3.2 Integration of traditional structures

Farmers might experience the traditional forms of labor exchange in the countryside as supplementary or primary components of projects. Consider a project whose objective is to reforest to decrease erosion. The peasant is already aware that he will utilize trees that can generate income for farmers and their families. The agronomist organizes training for these farmers in the multiplication of seedlings in nurseries, selecting the most qualified individuals based on their level of education to receive and share this training. However, he fails as only those who received training achieved the required outcomes.

The agronomist alters strategy and requires traditional groupings or "columns" to appoint one delegate in each column for the project. Techniques and technologies are spreading among the groupings because of the delegates' efforts. In this case, we notice the community phenomenon on two levels: the conventional level, which is more commercial, and the level of the project itself, which is more social; when these two levels were combined, they contributed to the creation of a larger common space.

Based on the columns, it appears that the project accepts their asymmetrical structure. However, it provides everyone innovations whose perceived good impacts will inevitably grow progressively over time. This does not presuppose the necessity for broader legislation by the agro-land reform, a third level that is unquestionably more political.

ADDITIONAL CONSIDERATIONS

Agriculture and the peasants are the foundations for Haiti's growth, based on the population size, since they constitute the accumulation base, and because they connect upstream and downstream with the entire society and economy. Therefore, it is fair to develop a ten-year strategy.

A program based on a decade

Only if there is a real political will can an economic program be implemented to stabilize the agriculture sector and prepare a recovery for the twenty-first century to be implemented. This should result in daring choices like

- reinstallation of specific commercial barriers;
- the closing, reorganization, or sale of underperforming government entities;
- legalization of land occupations and restructuring of agricultural land;

- reorientation of the public administration as a genuine public service as opposed to a predatory state;
- redefinition or redesign of work or duties of public service employees with corollary clearance through a productivity audit with an annual evaluation grid by employee and by unit; and
- ensuring the local liberalization of speech and action to enable the reorganization of civil society.

These essential and quick actions are a must for a genuine economic recovery to commence. This posed in advance, the agricultural and agribusiness sector's resurrection will require modest stages in both time and space. There are too many regional disparities, agroecological conditions, and socioeconomic factors for valid actions to be implemented everywhere for everyone and in every sector.

It is thus important to move in stages—with a thorough examination at each stage, based on the findings of these diagnostics—and to try on a modest scale improvement method whose expansion will always consider the particulars of each case. In other words, it is necessary to imagine two phases that can characterize most of the nation's action:

> ➤ Less than five years in the future
>> At the national level, we will use this time to ensure the protection of the internal market (establishment of customs policy) and to prepare the implementation of land policies and recapitalization, establishing framework legislation such as that proposed in the spirit and letter of the constitution in chapters dealing with the economy and agriculture (articles 245–252) and the environment and local authorities (sections 61–87.5). However, we advocate the formation of pilot projects to assess the modalities and effects of applying these initiatives at the local level.
>>
>> District-level recapitalization programs, if any, require reorien-

tation. Taking into account the opinions of farmers should inspire and promote a synthesis of regional knowledge, the outcomes of development experiences for the entire nation, and notably a redefining of the aims of each institution involved in the development of agriculture.

This strategy will have clear and limited effects in terms of output growth during this period, but it is a preliminary, essential, and required step (but not sufficient) to restore the agricultural sector.

➢ During midterm (five to ten years)

This is to guarantee the progressive adoption of land policy and recapitalization measures at the local level, as mentioned previously. This time will be characterized by a quickening of the tangible recapitalization of exploitable farms and a greater understanding of the agricultural landscape, which will allow for more stringent control and more efficient use of help.

This agenda is inconceivable without the assistance of a democratic, freedom-respecting, and development-promoting state. The rule of law is essential, and the future envisioned for our agricultural and peasantry will enhance it.

At this pace, market laws in open economies are not withdrawn; rather, they are modified to the economic realities in Haiti, which affects more than three-quarters of the population. It is the option of the great majority of excluded Haitians to reintegrate into the economy, society, and history of the country because of constant familial, social, and land conflicts. In the present years, Haitians should make this decision. Inviting them is the progress of the global world. And considering the constitution of 1987, which makes decentralization and participation the pillars of participatory democracy through local authorities, we advocate for successful decentralization that generates significant decisions that engage national life.

At this juncture, the central government will need to establish new institutional institutions to mentor and assist local governments that can achieve constitutional obligations.

These support, harmonization, and articulation structures created at the central level must coevolve with local and regional communities to achieve a national, decentralized, and powerful nation that serves the Haitian people.

We propose the formation of an Institute for Decentralization and Regional Development to replace the expired Direction of Local Authorities of the Ministry of the Interior with departmental councils as stipulated by the constitution. This institute will, for instance, be responsible for analyzing and proposing the establishment of institutional mechanisms of coordination between the central government and communities involving all members of civil society in national politics.

We must have the courage to reinforce the false choice of our past. We must maintain an open mind; we must avoid dogmatism and keep everything... simple!

CONCLUSION

It is quite uncommon to discover sophisticated and developed nations that have not achieved the needed equilibrium between their diverse economic sectors. Thus, several global studies have demonstrated the tight connection between underdevelopment and subsistence agriculture or "development and agricultural self-sufficiency."

Agriculture is seen as a source capable of satisfying at least the biological minimum and essential needs of the people for any country, a precarious minimum in most nonindustrialized nations. Now, as Haitians, we recognize the need to develop, in tandem with an industrial dynamic, an agricultural economy based on the population's immediate needs.

Thus, the bread and steel civilizations should evolve in tandem to maximize the use of resources in developing nations and to make the complementarity of various economic fields a necessary condition.

It is noted that the traditional characteristics of Haitian agriculture (e.g., gleaning or subsistence agriculture, absence of agricultural techniques, or use of archaic techniques) are obstacles to the sector's development.

Historically, the Haitian countryside was influenced by a fierce fight for access to land, which was likely the direct cause of various alliances, disputes, and even wars. Thus, a certain sawtooth growth is determined, bringing together, on the one hand, absent landowners and, on the other hand, sharecroppers who are disinclined to make the most of land that is not theirs. This lack of motivation is the first negative aspect inherited from the past.

The period from 1950 to 1980 was thus characterized by a quickening of the decline of the peasant economy, which affected the whole rural population and its general level of life and accelerated its proletarianization by limiting their access to productive resources and farmland. In addition, the migration of a substantial portion of the labor force to cities and other countries, along with a growing malaise in rural regions, was one of the causes of the deterioration of our agriculture.

Due to the steady and rapid growth in demographic pressure, the problem of unproductive ecosystems has caused major disruptions in the industrial fields, tools, ecology, and cultivable farmland. These crises manifest themselves in many ways. They are the result of constant and conventional factors such as

- a reduction in farmland due to the absence of an agricultural zoning policy;
- rarity of labor even nonspecialized that turns to more remunerative work;
- outdated agricultural practices that cause production loss;
- climate-related challenges, including droughts, storms, and cyclones;
- insufficient financial resources to enhance the sector;
- apathy or abandonment of farms because of inadequate compensation;
- cadastre is lacking in most of the country;
- gaps in public records and their persistent flaw; and
- repeated and alleged land disputes.

These are the fundamental parts of the dilemma of Haitian agriculture, which has been the focus of several seminars and conferences where professionals of diverse orientations have sought the most appropriate answers through brainstorming sessions circumscribing the many facets of the problem.

To enable the sector to fulfill its vocation and to mitigate the disastrous effects of the estate (succession)—effects that exacerbate land conflicts in the Haitian countryside—we must put more emphasis on the progressive development of the peasant economy rather than promoting foreign investment and the capitalization of small agricultural exploitation.

In fact, the gradual self-directed development that aims for the prioritization of local resources and productive forces requires the training of professionals who are not only able to conduct specific research on, among other things, the opinions and attitudes of farmers regarding the restructuring of rural areas in an effort to stem the exodus, experimentation, and adaptation of farming techniques but are also able to properly engage in the concerned area.

Therefore, neither the degree of foreign investment nor the parachute of equipment and procedures (which have nothing to do with Haitian reality) will rescue Haitian agriculture from its current predicament. Emphasis should be made on the training and motivation of farmers so they can better manage the technical, economic, and social aspects of their agricultural resources. They should not disregard the implementation of cooperatives apt to respond to stakeholders' first needs.

While it is true that a deplorable malaise disrupts Haitian agriculture to the point where it has a significant impact on the national economy, it is quite certain that the restructuring of rural areas, which focuses primarily on an organizational effort geared toward the establishment of specific organizations aimed at providing effective support for the rural population and for its own development, will offer the greatest potential for success.

The resources are abundantly available as are the remedial elements. It is now the obligation of each individual and the patriotism of others to refute the terrible phrase of economist Rony Durand that "Haitian agriculture is in the Pharaonic stage" to reestablish this country in its first vocation as an agricultural country. Certainly, it is regrettable that our forces are disintegrating due to internal conflicts.

Even though laws enacted by the administration of Emperor Dessalines on the census or the formation of private law and public law laid the groundwork for a stable government in a former slave colony, they were unable to modify the warlike mentality of the Haitian people.

While the rulers attempted to deceive the envious and while the real issue at civil insurgencies in the country was the struggle for power, the farmer did not notice a change in his pariah status on land conquered by arms. Imperceptibly, it came to be relegated in the old cabinets this freedom and independence that was dangled as the sole source of the social contract—freedom and independence yet won with blood and tears.

It should be remembered that the spirit of social defense existed until the ordinance of 1838—an ordinance that also contributed to weigh down our progression. How could French law adopted by President Boyer facilitate our evolution?

We acknowledge that the civil code was used as a suppletive law for our inadequate legislation in all areas where Haitian law was silent. But was this a justification for applying the dowry system to marriage contracts when Haitian customs do not recognize it? Shouldn't it have been preferable to organize the urgent "property regime" at that time?

Add to all our laws additional laws, but without the stability of lived experience, they will not alter the habits of the people, or they will stay without force, or they will be paralyzed.

In addition, how can we account for the nature of things such that, as Montesquieu asserted, the rules are the relations that result from the nature of things? It is a communal structure that was acknowledged in Africa, where the great-grandparents of Haitians originated. What is the

French civil code if not a combination of rules that legitimize the principles used in nations with written law and those with customary law?

The adoption of the French civil code was the most detrimental and inopportune of all our imports since it was not necessitated by need. However, laws are the offspring of need. The awkward legislator's efforts to import made institutions into this new country vain. These laws do not shape the mentality of a society. We fall to the profusion of memories but only behind a mountain of feeble imitations of our old masters' masterpieces. We "bend" beneath the weight without a flicker of optimism that guarantees the country's future.

Isn't the "becoming national!" ought to be the topic of our continual eyebrow toward all the strange and exotic components, all the wogs who stroll our sidewalks? Would it not be a cause for concern if undesirables from other cultures united to threaten our security?

Therefore, rid our imperial, royal republican constitutions. Rid our future constitution of all slag, which is generated and which plague so many times the application. Save the rural world. Save our beloved country, Haiti!

In the meanwhile, though, who will discover a new mystique to remodel the beam to preserve our independence? In the absence of a national consensus, it is futile to think that institutions and laws by themselves could promote democracy and the emancipation of the Haitian people.

"We are travelers seeking our homeland; we must not wander aimlessly; we must look up to find our way."

Out of the African bush, living nearly three centuries in the hell imposed by France through its slave system in Saint-Domingue, to ascend after an epic war with the mighty French army to the pinnacle of glory to create a nation after having given birth to a mixture of Spanish, English, and French elements, such is the martyrology of our nation, the origin of its remarkable destiny.

If united sorrows, anguish, joy, and will may establish a nation, it is vital to maintain it in a constant state of defense that keeps it alert and prevents it from becoming complacent in a false and apparent. We must look up to determine our direction.

BIBLIOGRAPHY

Books

Anglade, Georges. *L'Espace Haïtien.* Presses Universitaires du Québec, 1944.

Bertin, Etienne. *Cours de droit civil français.* Imprimerie et Librairie Générale de Jurisprudence, Paris, 5è édition, 1918.

Budeau, Georges. *Le libéralisme.* Editions du Seuil, 1979.

Constantin M. Paul Aeta Verba. *Imprimerie des Antilles.* Mai, 1982.

De leusse, Jean-Frederic, Xavier Pillot, Yves Rolland, and Jean-Baptiste Toulouse. *Finances Publiques et Politiques Publiques,* Economica, 1987.

Deronceray, Hubert. "Sociologie du Fait Haïtien." *les Editions de l'Action Sociale.* Port-au-Prince, 1976.

Deshommes, Fritz. *Néo-libéralisme: Crise économique et Alternative de Développement,* 2nd Edition. Presses de l'imprimerie II, 1995.

Fanfan, J. E. *La Recherche de la Paternité.* Bibliothèque Haïtienne, 1944.

Fouchard, Jean. *Histoire des Idées Politiques.* Presses Universitaires de France, 9è édition, Septembre 1985.

Janvier, Louis-Joseph. *Les Affaires d'Haïti (1883–1884).* Paris Flammarion, 1885.

Micheline, Labelle. *Idéologie de Couleur et Classes Sociales en Haïti.* Presses de L'Université Montréal, 1978.

Monteil, Bernard. *Principes de Management.* Les Presses de l'Université du Québec, 1981.

Moral, Paul. *Le paysan Haïtien.* Les Editions Fardin, 1979.

———. *Le Paysan Haïtien: Etude sur la vie rurale en Haïti.* Paris, 1961.

Ricci, Jean-Claude. *Introduction l'Etude du droit.* Hachette livre, Paris, 1993.

Romain, Jean-Baptiste. *Quelques Mœurs et Coutumes du paysan Haïtien.* Imp. De l'Etat, 1959.

Spencer, Milton. *Contemporary Microeconomics*, 6è édition. Worth Publisher Inc.: Janvier, 1986.

Salgado, Antoine. *L'Adultérin devant la société.* Ed Panorama, Port-au-Prince, 1964.

Codes

Duvalier, François. *Code Rural.* 1963.

Matard, René. *Code de procédure civil annoté.* Presses de l'Imprimerie Le Natal, Juin 1981.

Menan, Pierre-Louis. *Code Civil Haïtien annoté*, tome II. Presses du D.E.L, Port-au-Prince, Septembre 1995.

Nicolar, Léger. *Code Civil.* 1965.

Pascal, Trouillot E. *Code de lois Usuelles, Tomes I et II revus et corrigés.* éditions Henri Deschamps, 1990.

Courses

Martial, Célestin. Cours de droit rural 2è année.

Gervais, Charles C. Cours d'Histoire du droit.

Fièvre, Michel. Cours de droit civil 2è année.

Grégroire, Eugène. Cours de droit civil, Iè année.

Newspapers

Bulletin de l'institut Haïtien de Crédit Agricole et Industriel—Banque de l'Etat haïtien, exercice 55–56.

Haïti Journal, 15. Janvier: 1940.

Haïti Coop, nos. 9–10. Décembre 1998.

"Le Concubinage face à la législation, la revue juridique et culturelle," nos. 22–24. Juillet, Août et Septembre 1982 par Arthur V. Calixte.

"Comment cesser de cultiver la pauvreté en Haïti." *Nouvelliste du.* Mai 20, 1998, par André-Yves Cribb.

ABOUT THE AUTHOR

Nixon A. Charles is a professional with experience in various fields such as management, teaching, and real estate. He holds an MBA from Nova Southeastern University, a bachelor of law from the State University of Haiti, and a BS in International Management from the American College of Switzerland.

In Haiti, he worked at the Ministry of National Education for nearly ten years, either as head of service or as advisor to a minister. In 2000, he abandoned the runoff of a legislative election because of gross irregularities and illegitimate maneuvers orchestrated by the Haitian administration of the time. At the end of the nineties, he was the spokesman of a group of executives and employees of the Ministry of National Education who, after intense and lively negotiations, led the Haitian government to understand the need to create and to contribute to the very first health insurance program for all employees of the Haitian public administration. He is a founding member of the Cooperative d'Epargne et de Credit, which produces financial services to thousands of stakeholders in Petite-Rivière de l'Artibonite.

He currently lives in Florida where he teaches math and provides consultation in the financial field.